Last Stanza Poetry Journal

Issue #6:
The Elephant in the Room

Edited by Jenny Kalahar

Jeffrey Spahr-Summers, artist

Stackfreed
Press

Andrena Zawinski's "Haiku, Driving from Pescadero" was previously published on *YourDailyPoem.com*.

Alden Wallace Mackay's "Beef on the Side of the I5" was originally published in *Endless Nights*, his collection of poetry.

Michael H. Brownstein's "Ota Benga Told Me These Things in My Catcher of Dreams" was previously published in *Moristotle* and *Medusa's Kitchen* as part of a sequential collaborative work.

Anders Carlson-Wee's "The Mattress" and "New Place" originally appeared in *Virginia Quarterly Review*. "Footprint" originally appeared in *New England Review*.

Judy Young's "Vacation" was originally published in her collection titled *Wild Wood*.

The Elephant in the Room.

The striking cover image by Jeffrey Spahr-Summers inspired this theme, and as usual, writers could take the prompt in two different ways. I asked poets: "What in your life is large and obvious but never written about or that you've studiously avoided writing about? What have you always felt wasn't worth writing about, although a significant part of your life? What are you silent about that you might benefit from writing on and sharing?" Another take was to write about elephants—real, imagined, stuffed, historical.

These stanzas are chock full of emotions, dark and hard as coal, or moldering and gnawing at these pages, ready to bite, crumble, or both.

Take care while reading—the feet here are heavy, and not all elephants wear bells in their ears to warn of their approach.

Jenny Kalahar, editor

On the Spectrum

If, when you first meet me, I make a slight bow
or curtsy for curt moments, you may see how,
because I've so rarely been taken up in
any other's hands, it won't disappoint me
if you seem not to notice how much private pain,
with little else at my command, flows in,
usually, against almost everyone's
ominously oblivious observations.

Although I've always had so little to say
about the conditions to which I'm subject,
struggling with words, machine- or heartbeat-piqued,
a language with which we'll likely never connect
at intersections of our ways of being,
sometimes I might try to give you back something
in courageous exchange—but it may seem strange,
like a box inside a box, wrapped up, intact—

or just another daily miscommunication
quite easily ignored. Yet, if all these plain
coatings of fears of others are to protect
my own begrudging of a trying to please,
I only seem harder to deal with because
I'll always have the energy to maintain
all these continuous superficialities.

David Schloss

The closer they approach with dangling ropes, beating
sticks against pot lids and shouting her name, the deeper
she plunges into the forest into which she flees, indifferent
to the cuts and bruises she suffers to her bruised skin,
her thunderous voice cracking like the splintering branches
she pushes aside. She will live off the land, befriend owls,
and study the stars glimmering in the sky. Oh, such beauty!

She has lost a friend—it has been explained—another of
her kind. She is grieving and beside herself. Let her
roam, we are told by the handler, and stay out of her way.
As predicted, she emerges three days later, drawn close
by a hooting truck horn and its lights piercing the darkness.

She reaches slowly with her hesitant, arching proboscis
for the clump of fresh, purple turnips the handler offers.
Soon she'll be ready for loading, ready for the whining road.
Inside the dark trailer, the slow vibration will make her doze.
She will dream of her absent friend. She will dream of Agnes.

David Vancil

Elephants in Tall Grass; or, VC Elephant Hunt
Vietnam, 1969

We dive straight down toward the jungle.
The paths of the enemy's elephants cut through
the tall grass, displaying sublime patterns
which spiral outward before they disappear
into nothingness. Where are they now?

Yelling into our headsets, the recon pilot
and I speculate over the thrumming engine
that they're hulking under the thatch
of trees at the base of the mountains
which they crossed as if generaled
by Hannibal bringing supplies. Like
a fifth columnist, I pray they're never found,
for I know the pilot, eyeless behind his visor,
would not be deterred from wreaking havoc,
nor would I dare to stop him. This is war, or so
we've been told. There are many victims.

A sudden glint in the northwest draws my eye,
and I advise the pilot through the roar
of the plane's engine of my find. He nods
and dives, strafing and firing his rockets,
into shiny silver, disappointed it doesn't blow
and by the absence of devastating light.
"Heading back," the pilot barks. "Roger," I reply
into my helmet mouthpiece. After an hour,
we have found only faint hints, but pretend
we are satisfied with our so-called intelligence.
I am glad we did not find any of the elephants.

David Vancil

Across from the Deaf School, Austin, Texas

The smiling woman folding her underwear
points to my nose, smirking at the paper tissue
stuffed into my nostrils. She holds her head
between her palms and makes the face of *The Scream*.

The wind gusts and spores of cedar seed splatter
against the plate glass window, trying to get in
like the zombies of *Night of the Living Dead*,
but in putrid green instead of sinister black and white.

We laugh in pantomime as we fold unmentionables,
widening our eyes in mock horror. Oh, so scary.

As I fold my whites, shirts, and jeans, she heaves
her woven basket onto her abdomen. She seems so tiny.

She soldiers forth. At the door, she glances back to nod.
I wave as she steps into the maelstrom.

David Vancil

The Woman in the Moon

As a consequence of lost love,
a woman moved to the moon,
where she lived in a crater
and gnawed its gray gravel.

She neither disdained the earth
for its green good nor called
to her lost lover. Instead, she gazed
below, content he'd never know
her beauty, never know her love.

Still, he lived on just the same,
a man with wife and children.

And if sometimes he marveled
at her eternal beauty through
the gauze of night and felt
old stirrings, he would laugh
and tell himself he'd grown daft,
a foolish dreamer. She must
be the same as I, he believed,
her teeth gone bad in her jaw,
nothing left to chew with.

Let her play tricks with light,
let her make her long shadows.
Let her loom in the darkness
and hide in daylight, disturbing
his dreams. Let the tide rise.

David Vancil

The Battle for Baguio, the Philippines

Father shot an enemy dead, Mother said. Wounded,
he languished in a hospital with pretty nurses
and lived. Sometimes Mother said he cried out
in his sleep, dreaming of the Japanese lieutenant
who'd stared back at him from his foxhole.

But Dad held his past close like a poker hand,
never revealing himself to me. He played golf,
one of the guys within a pastoral setting, never home
except to sleep it off or watch our small TV.

When I was a kid, we watched *Have Gun—
Will Travel* sitting side by side. He liked
the man in black with the thin moustache
and the ivory knight adorning his holster.
When I grew older, we watched *Bonanza*.

David Vancil

religion is the logjam of our lives,
the mysterious and crazy secret
people whisper to each other
over the din of reality

bless us oh lord
as we lie in the field of alone
the sky glittering
and empty, the darkness
a blanket as the cold sniffs
at our feet.

take up the empty space
between me and the river,
buffer the mountains and the void
of the sea, hold me in forever
let me bask in the resonance
of companionship

                              Mary Sexson

Last Wishes

I don't want to be dead somewhere.
Not where they can see me
all dressed up in some outfit
I would never wear.

Not somewhere
with my hands folded nicely
on my chest like I'm praying
which I never do. Just put me

on the pyre. Make sure I'm gone.
Strike the match, light me up.
Sit close, like I'm
the best fire you've ever built.

Get warm and tell a story.
Let the flames light up the sky.

Mary Sexson

Little Motherland

Who could know the loving deeds
of friends meant so much?
Who could know the sisterhood
of mothers hidden in plain sight?

In the Kinder years, time was elastic,
stretched thin with worry
and not enough hours in the day.
The friend who came to help at
children's parties with big bags of crisps,
all Tiffin Cake and tolerance.

Who listened as you whimpered into
a tea towel about your lack of sleep,
patiently pointed out "Baby is only eight weeks
old and *this is normal.*"

Who made many cups of tea, the kitchen
conversation backlit with interruptions
and cries of various hues.

Who took interest in your children,
smiling joy at their achievements like
the Abuela who wasn't there.

Who knew the ins and outs of family dramas
that you laughed at together while your
face told a darker tale.

She lent you a good suitcase on wheels
for a work trip so you could look the part.

She shared a cloak for you to hide
under until you could present yourself
to the world again.

She became a little mother to you.
For a while, your love seemed skimpy recompense
for one who had saved your life in the trenches.

Who could ever know that when she went,
this sister-in-arms left you wailing
like the motherless child you once were,
a long, long way from home.

Jacky Pugh

Lost Boy

From the tiny fingernails
I bit off while feeding him
to the "Speak to the hand" years
of surly, not quite boyhood,
more boyz-in-the-hood.

His little hand in mine,
walking slowly up the hill.
Boyskin becomes the hand that slams
the door, punches the bag until knuckles raw,
paints the sea red, sprays blackbirds
of unhappiness on white walls,
scribbles over photographs,
crossing himself out.
He's written, "When there's nothing left to burn,
you have to burn yourself."

Funny little boy who went to
Playbox for a whole year dressed as
Superman, red knitted patches
when his knees wore through,
now walks in Macbeth shoes holed
below the waterline,
paint-stained hoody,
jeans—the same pair, the same pair,
the same pair, day after day.

A piggyback down the hill to
Waterstones at midnight bought
the latest Harry Potter.
Read nightly chapters squashed together
on the Van Gogh bed.
He watches *Celebrity Come Dine with Me,*
draws a hand in his artbook, then another.
Lurks in the garden, smoking,
keeps strange hours and habits,
laptop open, constantly texting.

The school photos smile down from
their vantage point on the piano.
Home is gone. It is a place
to rest at night and scramble over
the rubble to get to work or college.

I want to run away in a white van.
I need a scarf of love and
socks of wisdom, my armour against
the invisible attacks, hidden enemies, and
IEDs that lie under the floorboards.

Jacky Pugh

Driving away from the hospital at two a.m., it is striking how beautiful this old city is without makeup. The blacktop is rain-slicked and pure, Commercial Street's candlelight processing toward an invisible horizon. On the main arteries, occasional cars blink back in the rearview while the town is a patchwork of light and dark under clouds that reflect and refine the darkness. I'm OK with darkness.

It reminded me of that poem I wrote for you when we were young:

When I look into the infinity of your eyes
When I hold your hand:
      When our palms mix skin, blood, electrons
Maybe there is something else
      Something I can hold on to
      When the night is long.

I remember, we were together in the rain at Roads End. The waves— wind beating onto the beach in a conflagration of foam. Rain popped on our hoods while you held me, your arms shivering under my jacket. In that moment, that moment, with everything swirling, you calmed me, and we were an island among the elements. That storm is just like everything else I guess, every day.

Now your purse and watch are in the passenger seat, and I am almost home.

Marc Janssen

Call me *Michael*. I'm two hundred and fifty pages from the *Moby-Dick* finale. The flotsam of the southern seas chronicling my wake. Queequeg's facial tattoos. Stubbs' ubiquitous pipe. The lethal ironwork of the harpoon. And throughout my nautical passage, the Leviathan has not yet stirred a rousing halloo from the crow's nest. Or an itch in the captain's ivory leg. Chapters proliferate, instead, on whale taxonomy and cetacean phrenology. A foreshadowing that flows into allegory. The gospel of an American Jonah. What would *Frankenstein* be without its modern Prometheus? Or *Beowulf* without a Grendel slayer? What if *The Pequod* sailed into Schrodinger's paradox? The killer of giant squids cowers beneath a polar ice cap or masquerades as a puffer fish in the Mariana Trench. Overwhelmed with page fright. I've learned the words *paraquat* and *diegesis* during my watch in the masthead. Did I stumble upon these nouns in the throes of one of Ahab's parables? Salvage them from the ravings of a villain's beatitudes? Or did I burnish my lexicon to enliven my passage through these doom-augured doldrums? Will I be alert enough to sound the breach before the Behemoth's waves break overhead?

Michael Brockley

The Painter Replies to the Young Composer

from "A Story About the Body," Robert Hass

I felt your eyes lust for what remained of my beauty while I brushed teal and indigo strokes across the canvas in our art class. The embryo of a new meditation on birdsong. I never thought I'd feel a man's chest pressed against my phantom breasts again. Until I sensed you counting my footsteps during a return to my cottage to dress for dinner. At the wine tasting, you waved an anthology of the thirty-six immortal poets of Japan, and I hoped to hear you read a senryu written by a woman with your coughing tiger voice. Or maybe Lady Ise's "Is this what you are asking me?" Instead, when I spoke of my mastectomies and our mutual desires, you cringed. And a shadow passed across the cowardice behind your eyes as you composed your excuses. I stepped into my loneliness again. And opened a window in my cottage to listen as the loons called to their mates while night fell upon the lake. Have you ever heard a woman weep? Have you ever heard a woman wail with the fog rising above still water? Bowing my head, I discovered bees scattered across the windowsill like unlucky dice. I swept the insects into a bowl I baked in a kiln in Albuquerque. At the bottom of the clay pot, I carved a Japanese ideogram before applying a cobalt glaze. I wish you better luck with the dead bees. You see I covered them with rose petals. You will have to figure out the *kanji* by yourself.

Michael Brockley

Upon Closing My Eyes at 20

everything in my head is a story
impaired
my mind is snipped at by scissors
until all that is left

of my concentration
are perfect paper dolls dancing furiously in circles
paper cuts on my index finger
sting from touching the white
smooth hands that clutch each other

entwined like barbed wire
a menace to real girls
ponytails hurt when mothers
brush and tug
tying ribbons that collide bright and out of place

eluding me as though I walk naked down a crowded street—
oh, what rests in my head—
I soar, as grease, which sweats
off sizzling bacon careening
off clouds in the clear night
clouds as soft to my skin as flannel

leaves float falling with the hurt in my head
while midnight's yin yang struggles
like the globe to turn in the sky

a brilliant breast dancing upon the center of the ocean—
round reflected
as candy in the eye of a child—

a bright smear in my mind
like cinnamon passing over the tongue
scalding sweet

I bite the moon
I am still hungry

At Dawn, 40-Year-Old Eyes Open

tumbling over to-do lists, I am alert as
a hand trying at a combination lock
    [like the safe we now secret filled
    with adult-type documents or
    like my daughter's first locker]

amazing all of these numbers
—fitting together in concert—
        open doors
    I did not think possible
as I went elbow over elbow
on my belly   metaphorically
under spiky barbed wire
avoiding friendly and unfriendly fire
bright and displaced

jolted awake by the old walking-naked-
down-a-crowded-street dream, again
—oh, what rests in my heart—fever
laced over my shoulders
[warm and soft like the green blanket
grandma bequeathed us]

    Young Girl, you couldn't know
that cinnamon will mellow in the bread
    that you will bake
for a family who will think
        you're the moon
that hunger will gnaw
like a fox worrying your black hen's neck
enough to find sustenance from her brain
like the cord that wraps
      through your body
generating an electric hum
      steady as molasses

you will greet the sun
you will not squint

Liz Whiteacre

Saturday's Child

She'll never sell out / She never will /
Not for a dollar bill. ~ Donna Summer

As Saturday's child, I did have to work hard for the money.
Cataloging the sale and return of department store garb
after being transferred on for not being what the boss called
his "hot tomato," a promotion dangled as a shared room
on a business trip, and for the first time learning to say *no*.

Pulling on a fringed bikini and knee-high boots to jump
from a bull rope onto a stage as a beachside go-go girl,
even after failing a bare-breasted audition. Cranking out
fish lures and offered pay under-the-table as the supervisor's
"pretty little bird to train" before flipping him off in a walkout.

Getting stiffed on tips waiting corporate parties, sweating out
mid-summer short orders of cheesy omelets and gooey pancakes
washed down with pitchers of bloody marys and mimosas.
Grabbed by the throat by a drunken pill-popping veteran
for shutting him off from another Long Island iced tea.

Editing grad students' papers on my high school education,
chasing them down for their extra change and fat checks.
Proofreading briefs, groped at the back, waist, hips, thighs.
Dropping out of a PhD program after A's turned into B's
for standing up the professor advisor at the local literary pub.

Teaching a boy to understand magnetism and constellations
who would go braindead quarterbacking, another to read
who would end up a ward of the court for crawling through windows
to open doors for her strung-out burglar father,
propositioned by the school's superintendent, quitting the job.

And, as the fortunetelling rhyme goes: Monday's child may be
fair of face, Tuesday's full of grace, Wednesday's with its woes,
Thursday's with far to go, Friday's loving and giving,
Sunday's bonny and blithe, but this Saturday's child
really had to work hard for a living—in more ways than one.

Andrena Zawinski

Haiku, Driving from Pescadero

fog blankets the road
lighthouse signals a warning
dunes and grasses blur

leggy coastal pines
bend beneath the weight of wind
falcon on the wire

Andrena Zawinski

I'm Going to Go to Work

I'm going to go to work.
Early morning,
chasing the sunrise.
At night,
under a shotgun moon.
Or maybe I'll swing
like shifting sands
in chunks of eights or twelves.

I'm going to go to work
because I wish to make no playground
of my idle hands.
Also,
because I like to eat.

I'm going to go to work.
Not for the joy of palaces built
or moving stubborn things:
rusted ratchets,
sledgehammers,
steering wheels.
I go for love.
For the simpler,
finer
pleasure
of going to home

Chris Hasara

Nanukatukitsukatsu

"What we've got here is failure to communicate."
~The Captain, *Cool Hand Luke*

"Don't you speak Ing-u-rish?"
~Mom

How to explain the difference between knowing and
knowing. Observe your hand and the slipper in it.

Despite love, despite anger, accept the consequence
of misdeeds and careless action, of playing hooky

and getting caught, of tracking in mud and ignoring
requests regarding matters trivial to a teen.

We never knew the literal translation of the word,
incantation, curse, or whatever it may have been,

and we certainly couldn't spell it, but the sounds
most definitely said "you in a heap of trouble now,

boy," but with a Japanese rather than southern accent.
Think Strother Martin, but smaller, feminine, Asian,

prettier, tougher, and confident in her message. Apply
the slipper to the miscreant's backside. Do this twice,

if not more. Say *"Mata, mata."* Shake your head.
Acknowledge affection and dismay. *Again, again.*

Robert Okaji

Not What I Planned

First of October, and leaves flame up red
on the big maple out back,

unlike in California where flames are real,
houses and wineries burning to dust, the dead

count rising daily. No, this flame
is metaphorical, and unfortunate when you stack

it up against the reality of climate change.
Doesn't it feel like the world is spinning

out of control, like God is smoking crack
in some basement, unable to claim

his kingdom or answer our prayers or even arrange
to have the fires put out? Toss in a cup of economic despair,

a cup of racial division, and two cups of COVID,
and you can't help but feel deranged.

This was going to be an autumn poem where I proclaimed
the beauty of dying leaves as they glow in the crisp air,

but it's turned dark; it's turned real.
Look, this world has been falling apart since the beginning,

but we've learned how to ignore the signs and stare
at the glorious sunset. It may be the only way to stay sane.

David James

Q And A

"Hedge wizards and makers of almanacs, UFO abductees and 5G truthers, all hold out
the same promise—that one universal hidden truth shall be revealed,
and the horror of not knowing will come to an end."
~ From "Complexity," Hari Kunzru, *Harper's*, January 2021

It's raining on December 21, and I don't know why.
Jupiter and Saturn align tonight
into what might have been the star
of Bethlehem, and maybe it was, but we'll never know.

Most days, I shake my head and sigh,
not sure what to do or what to believe.
The truth is a moving target, one moment in Qatar,
the next week in Detroit. Tomorrow, it's flying low
over Lake Huron before landing on the Isle of Wight.

Maybe there is no hidden truth and we've been deceived
by our own simplistic thinking. Maybe we
should consider the concept of truth like snow—
each flake unique and beautiful, each truth a sight
for sore eyes: the truth of fire and a Cuban cigar,
the truth of pumpkin pie, the truth of the acorn or flea
or red cardinal on a fence post on a snowy day.

Maybe truth is everywhere and nowhere. Light
shines down from the planets whether we're standing in the yard
or asleep in bed. The world performs, and we're in the show
for such a short time: be happy to grab any old truth and stay.

David James

One Lovely Day at a Time

Sitting in the back yard,
a cool breeze rustling the leaves,
the drone of an airplane above,
watching four or five cherry tomatoes slowly turn orange
on the plant,

and I forget the ease
with which it could all vanish,
swept away or burned, everything going black
with a massive aneurysm,

like my uncle who sits at home
waiting for his to burst and bleed out.
In some ways, I hope he has a heart attack
in his sleep—a quiet, quick departure.

How do you greet the new morning
knowing it could be a matter of hours or days
before your world goes silent?

I guess you savor this piece of toast,
enjoy that glass of grapefruit juice,
smile when your grandson
brings in a crayon drawing
of a mighty dragon
with your name
on it.

David James

Once Upon a Time

I was a PhD graduate student
at a prestigious Catholic university
when all my funds were cut off
and I lost the best fellowship for

a graduate student because I didn't
say, in an oral, enough words out loud,
on the spot, to a Kafkaesque question
asked by a dead serious professor

after my engagement to a girl I loved
went bust and I got a night job
at a liquor store where I had to keep
a can of Mace all summer ready

to spray if anyone tried to steal
from the till. Before I went to
work each night, I ate a pressed ham
sandwich and drank a glass of milk

and lost weight and refused to study
for my second oral exam in the fall,
but started instead to write the proposal
for my PhD dissertation on Robert Lowell

and the American Past because I could
not receive any moolah from that Great
Catholic University until Oral Exam # 2
and the thesis proposal were deemed

a success, as they were. Yes, there were hearty
congrats, and I gave thanks I didn't have to
head to the liquor store every night and maybe
run the booze dispensary all by my lonesome

with my trigger finger ready to push
on the Mace can if anybody else tried
to steal my future in academia. Now here
I am getting ready to pucker up my lips

to kiss the age of eighty if I last another couple
years after some thirty books published, half
of them collections of poetry, others prose
exploring my German American past.

Norbert Krapf

What the Body Does to Us in Time

Where does all the pain come from?
Those knobs at the base of the thumbs
that pulse and make it hard to open
anything screwed tight? And those noises
shoulder joints make when we lift
our arms? The dimming of our eyes
and disappearance of moisture
in them that once lubricated vision?

Those rude noises that more easily
escape apertures we'd rather
not name? And what about those
names that now escape us?
I mean, even of people we still know
we like. Oh, and those appointments
we are obliged to keep—who wrote them
down in such illegible script on the wrong
days or not at all, anywhere? And the sweet
flowers we have loved so long—why can't
they be polite enough to whisper their
euphonious names in our wide-open ears?

And love, why do we so seldom understand
what the other is saying and become irritated
by the irascible and too loud word *What*?
Why do our vowels still speak, but consonants
drop out of range so quickly though we strain
to hear their sounds? Why must you have
your eyes and I my ears checked so often,
those operatives we took for granted for so many
years but have so quickly and shockingly gone
goodbye? Why am I struggling to remember
what I'm trying to say? Who gave me the gift
of forgetting so much as fast as this?

Norbert Krapf

The Lost Child

You came out of the woods, crying.
The neighbor boy, the aptly named
Jason, little betrayer of souls,

led you in and abandoned you.
You found your way out
before we knew what had happened.

Not for the first time,
your resourcefulness saved you,
kept you from harm. I hope

that's the case now when you
have all but disappeared,
retreated into the distance,

become a memory.
Now we're the lost ones, wandering
the woods with no way home.

I want to come out of the woods,
to lose this falling-down grief
that keeps us from moving forward,

really, from moving at all.
Here's my hope: we'll both lose
whatever fear keeps us apart.

Peter Huggins

Three Senryu

Elephants

a mother and child
tears blinked away for eight hours
singing *baby mine*

Colonel Hathi's March

onscreen family
hup, two, three, four, keep it up,
two, three, four marching

The Elephant in the Room
or, untitled #6

now without speaking
forever ensconced within—
rapists never leave

                                    Alys Caviness-Gober

Alberta Bound

I own a gate to this prairie
that ends facing the Rocky Mountains.
They call it Alberta—
trails of endless blue sky,
asylum of endless winters,
the hermitage of indolent, retracted sun.
Deep freeze drips haphazardly into spring.
Drumheller, dinosaur badlands, dried bones.
Ancient hoodoos sculpt high, prairie toadstools.
Alberta highway 2 opens the gateway of endless miles.
Travel weary, I stop by roadsides, ears open to whispering pines.
In harmony North to South,
Gordon Lightfoot pitches out a tune—
"Alberta Bound."
With independence in my veins,
I am a long way from my home.

Michael Lee Johnson

Victimized by the Cat

A tendril of trepidation
unfurls inside me
as I let the cat out into the backyard at three a.m.
for the hundredth time this year,
a pattern I am mystified to have begotten,
signifying one more nail in my coffin
of chronic insomnia.

That's not the only thing
by which I feel victimized—
there is the aging of my body,
that persistent ache in my back,
and the slow ebb in the tide of my energy.
There is the tyranny
of the poorly timed traffic lights
and the pedantic pace
of the driver in front of me,
making me murderous.

This budding impotence could be amusing
if it were not suffused with rage,
if it did not bleed through
from a tiny girl inside with tangled hair
who climbed on the counter
for peanut butter and Wonder Bread, every day,
while her mother slept off her Great Depression
angled sideways, face down
on the bed she shared with the girl's father.
Even that could have been
simply a sign of spunk,
if food were the only thing
for which she hungered.

Being subjugated by ordinary events
might be humorous
if it did not emanate
from the terrorized look in the girl's eyes

at the vista of her drunken father's
apoplectic face,
bigger than all the faces
of all the bullies at school,
bent on some violence against her.

This tyranny by even the despotic house keys
that will not let themselves be found
would be funny,
if I were not nightly the tormented captive
of a Dark Man in a high walled prison camp
where disembodied arteries pour blood
that I cannot staunch.

Mary Kay Turner

The Last Elephant of Rome

He treads endlessly on marble slabs,
relics of Rome before the fall,
trunk and tail brushing the sad
iron bars of his imprisonment,
tracing ruts worn in rigid stone
by countless beasts before him
in expiation of their crime
of unfathomability.

For what man does not understand
he must confine or destroy.
In circuses and amphitheaters,
in numbers beyond calculation,
strange and wonderful creatures
were executed for fear and entertainment—
sometimes ten thousand in a single day.

In legend and folklore,
it is said that elephants never forget,
and memories are passed on
from generation to generation.
If that is so, what burdens,
what invisible chains must rattle—
they shackle the soul
of this final elephant …
or so he must think in his small world.
Alone in his despair and confinement,
he chuffs and rumbles and trumpets
to none of his kind.

But elemental Earth listens.
And Vulturnus, who blows day into night,
will never forget, or cease to measure,
the treacherous and hidden shoals of cruelty
and whisper the whirlwind.

Patrick Kalahar

The Elephant Celebes

Created by Dada Max
(died August 1914, reborn 11 November 1918)

Iron Behemoth, monster of the "war to end all wars,"
it lumbers toward Armageddon
on the metaphysical planes of de Chirico.

Metal legs with horrible, bloated metal body,
portholes belching yellowish poison
rotting souls and lungs.

The Elephant Celebes has two heads—
one for a future that it remembers,
the other for a past it has forgotten.

One head is at the end of a hose
that may be a trunk or tail or both.
The other head remains unseen. An enigma.

Startled fish fly through unlimpid air,
oblivious to or denying gravity,
searching for water in an arid land.

The Behemoth casts only a tiny shadow
because the sun, small and dim in the haze,
has misplaced the light of better days.

A headless mannequin dreams
of notions on a sewing table.
With nothing to say, she gestures

toward a metaphor that hangs
in defiance of reality
outside the painting's gilded frame.

Patrick Kalahar

Moderation

I.

Flew home from Israel
in week two of the Plague,
fourteen-day quarantine,
and my Zayde's haint
rasps "Idle hands ... Devil's friend."
So I'm painting our mange-
blotched 1940s Cape Cod,
our peeling white heart-haven.

Kibbutz Mizra, Plague day four,
I flail against the government's web.
Cancelled flights and shuttered stores.
In the Holy Land,
where the air rustles nervously
despite greening hills. And
there is no moderation.

The new order tells
my hotel to shed me
like winter fur in April.
But kindness prevails,
and I remain, fed even.
Anxiety forecast now
cloudy with occasional sun.

2.

Plague safety and painting
are best taken in moderation.
Six feet apart outside, but talk
sixteen feet up the ladder,
please, no farther.
Mental health jogging but
personal distance from step one,
rules too harsh, you rush,
overload the brush—

paint drips and spatters
on finished spaces.
And the virus persists.

Painting is meditation.
Smooth, silky brushes
caressing the clapboard.
Our house-skin now
sporting layers of ivory.

3.

Life and painting both
ninety percent preparation.
Wash, scrape, prime,
mask, wipe, scrub,
listen, think, act.
Zayde said, "Anything
worth doing is
worth doing right."

But I'll always have
spots to touch-up.

Gary D. Grossman

Rainbow, Brown, and Brookie

They are living rubies, emeralds, sapphires,
and opals rolled into one, sliding through
a cold riffle, holding where
insects drift downstream—
easy prey, just a quick snap.

Years stretch like old elastic,
and I have tired of them, baked or
wine-poached, sautéed in yellow
butter, decades of slick plates and
twisted skeletons, fleshless on
the communal bone china plate.
The scent of scales and crisp
skin wafting into the dining
room from our sun-colored kitchen.

So I bought a smoker.

That left flesh amber yet firm,
apricot-tinged, flinty, and
dry as Sancerre in July.

Every one I catch, I swear,
"the next one will go free."

Gary D. Grossman

Poem in Nine Parts

I

In early February as I mop the floor, I'm bothered to not know what PPE stands for or what is meant by an N95 mask. Siri, why doesn't NPR explain the acronyms they use? Good journalism uses the long form of a term at the beginning of a piece before using an abbreviation. It's your job to educate the audience. Don't assume they know or make them look it up.

II

Jogging the neighborhood on lockdown day two. The midpoint of the run is an empty uphill cul-de-sac that backs to a vineyard. Because fog feels especially isolating in quarantine, I dramatically call out "Hello!" to the hunched man pruning vines. He waves back but says nothing. I should have said hola, but wouldn't that have been presumptuous?

III

Replying to a Tweet from Nurya, the priest of Plainsong Farm, my thumbs type: *We may as well let grief sit quietly next to us on the couch, knowing we'll be better acquainted soon.* At two in the afternoon, I walk the dog past a man rarely seen at home, a Chinese-restaurant owner, Claire's dad. He's in a bathrobe, walking through his attached garage, taking out a tall white kitchen bag of household trash. In the fall at the middle school open house, I tried to meet Claire's parents, but we struggled with the language barrier and noisy hallway.

IV

A baby in a classic white bonnet and red pea coat (like a handmaid's mini-me) teeters back and forth between parents in the road on daily walks, falls on her bottom with regularity, gets scooped up. There is no traffic, and she doesn't yet know that the cracked blacktop is meant for cars. Weeks later in a hot pink parka, she's the only one gaining confidence amid COVID-19. Arms swing instead of bumbling outstretched, and stable ankles no longer test each step for balance. I throw wide the April window to congratulate her progress from a second-floor bedroom. Startled, she falls.

V

My cohabitants watch Hitchcock's cinematic trills while I watch the night hide a pink moon in a thunderous coat. In blinding pulses, purple-bright strings surge into crooked smiles. I see the next-door neighbor, a fifteen-year-old mom of a newborn son, skateboarding loops in the storm. She lets out the cat, then calls its name into the heavy rain, gives up, taking back inside the weighted draperies of her drenched hair and clothes.

VI

Nighttime dreams flourish—COVID-ignorant and pigment-rich. In sleep, human interaction is careless and unmasked, and so we wake with slowness. We rise for what? God: she has become the buffalo on the east wall print that takes my gaze each unalarmed morning.

VII

My housemate sips a two-liter of root beer through a metal straw. I sit on the sun-warmed driveway sewing masks by hand, and the drone hovering over me is not, in fact, controlled by some unsupervised kid but that dad over on Leelanau Street. Get that thing out of my f***ing airspace. I own all this—sidewalk to heaven. I will not be both quarantined *and* surveilled, not even for Big Gretch.

VIII

Another housemate wears a grey fleece blanket as clothing deep into the day, noshing waffles with Nutella (that she cannot prepare herself in her cold burrito state) and Klondike bars and watching TikToks at all hours of the day. Via text, I beg my best neighbor to spare a square of yeast packet to make pizza that I might smell rising dough. It's Ramadan, and I feel guilty mentioning food in the middle of the day, but I do it, nonetheless. Isra is, of course, gracious and generous, as is dinner.

IX

What is an issmuss? asks one schooled behind a laptop at the kitchen counter. I hear it as *-istmas,* the latter part of the winter holiday. *No, isthmus. The Isthmus of Tehuantepec.* There are so many words and so many geographies and so many languages left to be found outside of this dishwasher, this dirty spoon.

Anne Marie Holwerda Warner

I Am Waiting

I am waiting for someone to tell me
that, decades from now,
we'll still have our home, this earth,
that the wooded paths
will still abound for walkers.

I am waiting for someone to tell me
that seasons will behave:
the petrichor of the maiden monsoons
will not have turned mythical,
or poking the white wintry earth
won't have become a lost habit among little beings.

I am waiting for someone to tell me
that words won't remain vacuous cartons for long,
that someone will turn around
to infuse in them truth, honesty.
That language will breathe again.

I am waiting for someone to tell me
that we will someday learn to shun the unloving,
to know when and how they set us up for failure,
to stop giving them the benefit of doubt,
that we'll survive calling them out.

I am waiting for someone to tell me
that we shine peerless
in our undertakings, rejections, and re-risings,
that our tales, though matte-finished, need to be told.

I am waiting for someone to tell me all these
because I could never tell them to myself
or believe my own words.
Like elephants, they have sat too long
in my otherwise empty, expansive mind.

Mahasweta Baxipatra

43

Black-Eyed Susan

Susan ain't a bit finicky.
She don't do much complainin'.
That gal knows what she wants and needs,
which ain't much.
She's purposeful by design
and bound to get it done in spite of ya.
I've seen her pulled out by her roots
and set in the corner, left all day
without a drop a water.
She'll make do.

Oh, she might give ya a little droop just to make her point,
but give her a little lovin', a little nurturin', and that girl will rally.
She'll forgive you right quick for all your trespasses,
your failure and abandonment.
Your ignorance.

'Cause Susan is all about joy—
pleasure so real you can 'bout touch it with your fingertips.
Jubilation that unfolds in front of your eyes,
clutchin' her own heart till she's good and ready
to turn it loose, openin' and transformin' into brazen prettiness.

Susan ain't too complicated.
Every one of her slender curves is simply flawless.
Her color is brilliant like the sun, genuine and sunshine warm.
Her homespun petals in hues of shockin' yellow
circle that big ol' dome, one seedy dark eye
all sittin' there on top of that long, skinny stiff neck.

That woman will make you so happy
yor liable to throw rocks at the other flowers.

'Cept the roses, of course.

Theresa Timmons

Dallas

The Trinity once brought
slave-picked cotton
into the city,
and then slave descendants
to process the bales.

The Trinity was
the murky ribbon
that flowed a division,
keeping us in our place
when all was black and white.

The Trinity took my father,
washed him away
and Gramma's place
up the shore,
the same house that
survived lesser rains,
modest gulley-washers
that would chase us
up the gutter-pipes,
waiting on the roof
for the river to settle back
into its banks.

I hated that place,
hated having to
shovel up the muck,
pull out
what the floods destroyed,
then mopping, scrubbing and
rescrubbing back to her
worn out floors.

The Trinity kept flowing,
and big D kept on growing—
they put up a levee
to protect the land

on the other side,
just past where I could
skip my dreams and stones
across muddy waters,
sinking to her depths.

We watched it flood,
we watched it recede,
and we watched
as the Father, the Son,
and these Holy Waters
turned their backs
to those who
needed them most

while tall white men
would climb the flood wall
on the other side
and note the great tragedy
flowing below them.

Michael E. Strosahl

Riding the Elephant

Thailand's Sin City glowed at night.
Neon signs lit Pattaya's streets packed
with American sailors, Marines
and European tourists seeking
drugs, booze, and unbridled sex.

I was there to report on
joint military maneuvers,
but was struck silly
by the maneuvers of
the "Buy-Me-Drinky" gals
dressed in schoolgirl uniforms,
plaid skirts, and light blue blouses.
They performed bumps and grinds
in club doorways, promising wild sex.

Scantily clad waitresses in the hotel lobby
knelt next to my chair, gingerly holding
cups to my lips as I sipped my drinks.
Outside, the streets sported cocktail bus pubs,
and older prostitutes called from darkened doorways
that hid their age-warped bodies, selling themselves
for a few Thai bahts or Yankee bucks.

I spent most of my time in my hotel room
writing about how that day's exercise went,
sending the story to my editors in Tokyo,
calling my wife half an ocean away,
and fending off a hallway hostess
who wanted to give me an hour of
"the best ever sexual deep massage."

In the hotel restaurant, I saw
a family with two children
and asked my interpreter
where they would go for fun.
Besides a few religious shrines,
where would a tourist in

Sin City take a child?
Even the beautiful beaches
swarmed with sex.

He laughed and drove me to a zoo
where children perched on baby elephants
led around a small circular track.
He was taken aback when I asked
if I could scramble atop one for a ride.
I didn't care about seeming silly and laughed
as I climbed up on Dumbo for what was
the highpoint of my trip
to Thailand's version of Sodom and Gomorrah.

David Allen

Remembering

For decades, I was
the elephant in the room,
jotting down what I saw and heard
when I attended trials and responded
to wrecks, fires, murders, and mayhem.
I typed up what I saw and heard,
and editors splashed the stories
across newspaper pages.

We were the community's memory.

I spent twenty years
reporting in the Far East.
On the fiftieth anniversary
of the War in the Pacific,
I interviewed scores of veterans
sharing their memories of those
harrowing, island-hopping days.

A decade ago, I retired
from newspapers and
threw myself into poetry,
remembering in verse
all I'd experienced
in a life full of words.

David Allen

Toby Tyler

"See the elephants, see the clowns,
see the county police shut the circus down!"

An editor once said my story ledes were pure poetry.
And I was on a roll in Fort Wayne in 1986.
I was responsible for kicking
the Toby Tyler Circus out of town,
and had tons of fun doing it.

The small-time circus
was slated to set up its tents in the city's
Coliseum parking lot.
But the penny-pinching pachyderm show had left
a path of collapsing bleachers and broken bones in its wake.

"If the circus is coming to town,
it better stop by an insurance office first," I chuckled as I wrote.

Citing lack of adequate insurance, the city balked and the one-ring,
sorry excuse for a great show searched for a new local venue.
It finally found a farm lot just north of the city.

"There was a bunch of midgets putting up a tent in my backyard,"
a bewildered man who rented a house on the property said.
The lot owner neglected to tell him the circus was coming.

About one hundred and fifty spectators saw
the opening act before police closed the circus down.
It left town that night.

So, yeah—I killed the circus.
And all the clowns, elephants, lions, tigers, and bears.

Oh my!

David Allen

Elephants on Parade

Like the Maharajah's howdah
minus the sway and glitter,
my bookshelves bear and display
the immense kindness and mystery,
the hulking sadness of their servile lives

Clowning on cue for Hoagland's circus stars,
martyred for Hemingway's sodden sportsmen,
sacrificed to Orwell's imperialist honor,
confounding Rumi's inspectors touching parts in darkness,
carrying a new Ancient World through the Alps

Across infinite pages honored and abused,
this most improbable of high-order living wonders,
lumbering even into a Raymond Carver workaday story
whose hero wearies of a mother, brother, son, daughter,
all hitting him up, their meal ticket and doormat

And so he dreams of childhood, high and free,
riding on the shoulders of his father, long dead.
"Elephant" is the title of the story.
The word appears once in fourteen pages—
enough to make it a love story

Dan Carpenter

Ever-Present Absence

I've no desire to own a Jaguar
any more than a jaguar
as transportation to impress my neighbor,
nor as a pet to scare him away.
Expense, trouble, sheer excess,
ostentation all our true faiths condemn
no shields against death, more likely deadly

yet to age without them
would be poverty in the soul sense—
not to raise my eyes from the café table
every single time a steel masterpiece
paused purring for homage at a stoplight,
not to possess knowledge there exists
an animal finer than any I ever shall see

I have shared my time on this planet
with humans I hunger to know
and some I ache to know from knowing,
not one of whom has lived
without leaving a taste
I'll savor always, into the darkness
owing and owning nothing

Dan Carpenter

Anything Will Do

Silence raises its hooded head,
    pungi and swaying
        will not be enough.

    Bury it
        with
            staccato chatter
            droning TV
            raucous lyrics
    with
        clicking heels
        honking horns
        strident siren

        with
            moaning wind
            grinding mower
            guttural growl

    Anything will do.

Else it will slither grassward,
        creep under doors and strike,
    embedding toxic
        introspection.

            Lorraine Jeffery

The Line that Holds Two Truths

My annual wellness check was meant to be
routine—some bloodwork and a questionnaire,
the customary poking here and there.
Then later came a voicemail left for me:

The doctor said he'd like to do more tests.
There is no cause to fear, I told myself.
I've always been a paragon of health.
(That's when I felt the weight against my chest.)

The follow-up was more or less the same.
I filled a plastic cup again, they drew
more blood and took some x-rays, too.
I asked the questions I supposed germane.

The line that holds two truths I can't forget:
Too soon to say its cancer—yet.

James Green

The Unknocked Door

For SWA, July 5, 1957 - September 13, 2021

Inching home in pain past curfew along an acorn-littered sidewalk,
too weary to cry and feeling small, the knot in my stomach competes
with the agony shooting through my ankle.
I gradually allow squares of golden light
from neighbors' windows to calm me,
feeling their unspoken welcome.
I know I can knock on any door, but something, as always,
prevents me from asking for help.

Resting below a streetlamp flickering with white humming light,
I imagine my four teenage brothers here—
protective, teasing, and, as always,
talking and arguing and laughing
about those things that matter least:
who's *it* for kick the can, *Star Trek, Twilight Zone,*
card games, Monopoly, the sand bar in the lake,
our dog, school, friends, and rock & roll.
I say the least of all, and I especially never reveal
that one of them is the enemy in their rank.

This enemy is the brother who finds me,
lifts and carries me a block to our worn wooden back door,
almost crying with relief that I'm home and will be okay.

He is offender and protector both.
His eyes, blue like mine,
shine and spark and burn with emotion,
but often too much of it.
Frustrated, as if he doesn't realize
he can knock on any door but mine to ask for help, himself.
Or, he does know, but something, as always, prevents him.

It is a spare thing to have in common,
but it ties us together, nonetheless.

Jenny Kalahar

57

What Elephants Can't Remember

Giants lined and gray and thundering,
or quiet, lying gently still in groups,
or running, trunks swaying to their own rhythms,
tusks white, curving toward the orange sun: the elephants

Elephants stand for hours or march for days,
remembering well the greenest feeding grounds.
They remember sons and sisters even long departed,
places where they've laid their dead.
They communicate low or high or silently,
a trumpet or a soulful glance, the elephants

Elephants grow old together, stay connected,
remember the sweetest tastes of life,
blow playful showers over muddy friends,
shed tears as you or I would do.
And, wandering slowly against a setting sun,
cast long, wide shadows once again. But elephants …

Elephants cannot remember these few things:
they can't recall the reason why the rain will fall or not at all.
They used to know why rivers dried, why grasses grew,
why darkness fell when they grew tired.
They used to know these things and more.
The elephants

Elephants once passed these stories as they rested,
told them when each day had cooled,
before sleep came while a glowing moon caressed.
But life grew harsh and hard and dangerous,
with sounds and signs and sights of man,
their few necessities now grow scant, and the elephants ...
the elephants forgot

Jenny Kalahar

Chorus Line

I was driving slow enough to notice symbology
and in the mood for poetry,
even if self-created
along a narrow Indiana road.

Cornstalks were a chorus line of skinny-legged,
rust- and dark-green ladies.
Some crooked elbows,
trying to match the others in kicks of wind.
Some waved drying hands,
a royal tremble rather than a how-do-you-do.
The chorus line, in this way,
conveyed both happiness and disappointment.
Withered cow cobs still hung on,
shy, aging children who refused to leave home,
clinging but too chubby
to successfully hide behind their mothers.

At the next stop sign, I switched on the radio,
slipping back into dull reality.
Imagination can do the oddest things,
and I was becoming too attached
to these cornstalk dancers.
I worried I might start hearing
both friendly calls and scoldings,
and cling to them too long,
withering in the autumn sun.

Jenny Kalahar

Vacation

A riot of cicada and katydids
screamed from the trees as
late August toasted the sky,
deep yellow dust in the lane,
powder fine between my toes,
the taste of it on my tongue.

Tulip poplar leaves turned golden
flutter gently to the earth,
signaling another squirrel season of
my father hunting in the woods.
His vacation timed to arrive as squirrel season opened.
A step back in time—
my father's time.
A time if you missed your game,
you missed your supper

I watched intently
where a curve hid the lane
in its deep green dimness.
He usually came that way,
stepping from the shadows,
no rush in his step,
his gun across his shoulders soldier-style,
hunting jacket hanging low.

I am the oldest.
It was my duty to hold the game
while he dressee it with a practiced hand,
hide and guts flung to the woods' edge
for the yellow jackets' feast.

Judy Young

60

Even Stuffed Elephants Never Forget

Lying on its tummy,
trunk outstretched facing our bed,
fuzzy gray memories flash.
Semi truck flying over bumpy asphalt highways
like a magic carpet.
Shiny coal black eyes
sparkle with old memories:
what we saw,
what we did.
A lifetime of adventure
for our baby elephant and us.

                                    Judy Young

Dear Old Dad

Dad's passed out on the sofa again, and
Mom takes a back seat in the other room.
My plans for the evening are shot.
I will take care of the children, fix dinner,
console Mom in her grief,
answer the phone,
make excuses for dear old Dad,
take out the trash,
put the kids in bath,
send them off to bed,
and call my friend to report that Dad is drunk again.
No one here talks of it, pretending that nothing is wrong.
I go on about my weary way,
get Pop to bed,
stay up half the night watching movies,
go to work in the morning,
come home to Dad on the sofa again and Mom alone in her room,
kids playing in the den.
It has started all over, and mums the word.
Tiptoe around and pretend that nothing is wrong.
Listen to Dad's apologies and go on with my night,
and hope for a better tomorrow.
I love you, dear old Dad.

LeAnn Jones

Ota Benga Told Me These Things in My Catcher of Dreams

I was the hunter of elephants—
I fed my village for weeks at a time—
but I made two mistakes:
I welcomed the men with no skin
and I did not die a warrior's death
when they killed everyone in my clan.
I fought hard and took many of them
before they captured me whole.
Why did they not kill me?
They told about lessons to be learned,
but they underestimated a hunter of elephants.

Strangely, it was a man without skin
who bought my freedom,
took me to his world
away from forests and glades
to a place of noise and metal.

Yes, I returned home,
but there was no one to return to.
Yes, they put me on exhibit when I came back,
these strange people gawked,
wanting to sit at the same table as me
and, yes, my teeth,
sharpened into canines,
frightened and thrilled them.

It's just that I missed the forest.
I was an elephant hunter, a great man of my people,
a provider and warrior—
how sad I could not return when I wanted.
In my soft unnatural bed
I dreamt of going home, finding a mate,
beginning a new clan—
wasn't I the hunter of elephants?
The Great War got in the way,
men with no skin fighting men with no skin
and I did not understand.

I could not die a warrior's death
I with capped teeth
living in a room without trees,
without brush.
This was no way to live—
the glory of teeth hidden from view,
dressed in clothing that chafed
skin and soul,
working in a large building,
making things of no intrinsic value.
So I let myself die—
the gun a weapon of my enemies
and in the battle to death,
I died a warrior,
the hunter of elephants.

There are many myths about me,
many more lies.
Remember me not
as the caged man in St Louis,
not as an exhibit in Washington DC,
nor as a man behind metal in the Bronx,
but as a man.

I was on view, I was an exhibit,
but I was never a slave.
Yes, I gorged on bananas,
yes, I bragged about my teeth,
yes, I snarled better than the lion nearby
yes, I knew how to put on a show.

I was the first performance artist,
but never a prisoner in a cage for long—
just enough to look into the faces
of men who could never outdo me.

Michael H. Brownstein

Remains of a Memory

The toy elephant in the room sits upon his bed,
a gray rumpled patchwork, tattered and torn.
Once its satiny material held a radiant sheen
that glistened in the night against his bedspread.
A birthday gift from his beloved grandmother,
it became my five-year-old son's confidant,
friend, and protector who slept with him.

I remember how he would look at me, smile,
and, laughing, say, "Look Mommy—elephant."
I would make up stories for him about his
patchwork companion, adventures of daring deeds,
journeys to faraway lands, or outer space.
He would act them out in the back yard,
and so his poor elephant had to be washed daily.

I miss those enchanted times, the muddy toy,
my son's laughter, and joy he gave to me.
Too soon shattered by tragedy, his life cut short,
the pain so sharp that broke my heart.
I pick up the toy elephant and weep again.
A memory left behind, now he's gone,
and with each year also becomes faded and worn.

Mary A. Couch

Listening to the Sounds

Listening to the sounds of his breathing,
she knows he has drifted off,
exhausted after several hours
of raging punching screaming kicking.

While she, naked on the bedroom floor again,
needs to pee
but dares not move
and risk waking him.

She lies shivering,
silently pleading for sleep that won't come,
feeling the pressures of the day ahead,
haunted by fears
of making a life-threatening mistake
with one of her patients.

She fantasizes about being one of them,
safe in a clinic,
surrounded by people
who would care for her
and cover her bruised, icy body
with a freshly laundered sheet.

                                    Delilah Bleu

Hiking on a Warm September Morning

Hiking a secluded wooded trail
on a warm September morning,
she's drinking the gold
of exuberant goldenrod,
grateful to be alive.

She stops to watch monarchs
light on purple thistles
where bumblebees feed,
and inhales the heady fragrance
of countless bushes covered with clusters
of tiny white blossoms.

Continuing on, enlivened,
she hears footsteps behind her
and turns to see a shirtless male jogger
beaded with sweat.

Abruptly, a wave of darkness
spreads through her.
Visceral sensations flood her body,
reminding her how quickly she can be crushed
by a mix of rage and aberrant testosterone.

After he passes,
her gut urges her to turn back.
He's the only person she's seen on the path today,
and she's a long way from the trailhead.

Almost thirty years since fleeing
the murderous madness
that nearly ended her,
she's still haunted by hypervigilance
and middle-of-the-night adrenaline spikes.
Guardedness and invisibility are integral for her.

Another inner voice,
one that longs for freedom
and a larger life, balks.
Obsessive self-protection
has kept her small.

Weary of projecting her fears onto her world
and unwilling to relinquish
the jewels of this moment,
she walks on,
her wariness in tow,

watching sun-filled goldfinches
dart from one brambly bush to the next,
and hearing songbirds trill melodies
that waft over the tightness in her throat.

She begins to hum.

                              Delilah Bleu

Family

It's a trick of love and chaos,
this emergence,

against the weariness of history
and the human mess—

the blood like death, the smell like dung—
into the midst of

careless romantics, horny children,
wards of the state;

the nest a clutch and vice versa,
these particular

children's games of pretend put on
for the world to show

how they're not so bad, how even
they could find someone,

at the same time grooming their
babies against it,

recruiting them witless into the fantasy,
revenge against

classmates who thought they were weird,
parents who wouldn't

let their kids play with them: stunt, deceive,
ill-prepare—adult

revelations ushering the snap,
strewing headlines and

grounds with "inexplicable violence
[...] in broad daylight."

Mark Henderson

At a Sudden Sound

The birds' departures
leave a language of doom—
dinosaurs once,

echoes of the comet
sending mantle to sky
in the approach

of squirrels and humans
alike, ancestral smell
in the breath of

machines—felt more than read
by sky-wary mammals
never raising

their heads, business noising
the air to keep out
a sudden sound.

Mark Henderson

Heart and Heartache

Without warning, my face has morphed into that of my mother's,
of my grandmother's.
Histories of heartaches track through my veins,
down to knees that ache.

Gravity relentlessly pulls,
as evidenced by the heart-shaped mole on my thigh
I was born with, now split in two:
a broken heart.

I am the creation of generations of grief,
untethered from the woman I was.
Only memories are left,
like sweet cake crumbs on a cracked plate.

I still live and love by the old songs,
still sometimes dance alone in my house,
ancestral loneliness working its way through,
letting out the hurt.

Kimberly Bolton

Going to See the Elephant

We stop the car on the side of the road,
climb out to get a better view.
We are standing where pioneers once stood,
facing west, eyes and hearts straining for sight
of that farthest hinterland across tall prairie grass,
yearning to go to see the elephant.

Old pioneers stood here, hesitating,
watching others go before them,
watching wagon trains make the great passage west,
feeling a deep heart-hunger to see it for themselves.
Here was everything they could need or want,
everything familiar, tried, true.

Out there were unknown things they longed to see,
heard of but barely imaginable:
an undulating sea of prairie grass thousands of miles wide,
gigantic mountain ranges with narrow passes and deep gorges
where a man might disappear and never be found again,
desolate deserts under a burning sun,
strange animals, odd flora and fauna.

They felt as we feel watching astronauts
stepping onto the surface of the moon
or contemplating a flight to Mars.
You can almost hear whispers in the dry wind
that sweeps through the low prairies:
Should we go? Should we stay?
Almost feel the lump in their throat as those hardy pioneers
hitched horses to covered wagons and began to roll west.
Going to see the elephant
they told those they were leaving behind,
perhaps forever.

Here we are, generations later, standing beside our car doors,
the same spirit of adventure moving through us.
We can almost see wagon wheels
carving their path into the earth,

long shadows stretching over prairie in the setting sun.
We return to our air-conditioned car, grinning at each other,
feeling the same deep-seated eagerness.
Wheels begin to roll west down the highway,
and we are off to see the elephant!

Kimberly Bolton

"Going to see the elephant" was an American idiom (although possibly much older in European lore), particularly during the great American migration west by way of the Oregon, California, and Mormon Trails in the mid-1800s. The adage underscored the American pioneer spirit as the covered wagons set out across the frontier, as well as the hardships and privations they would soon experience during the journey. "Going to see the elephant" expressed the spirit of human adventure and bravery in the face of adversity.

The Words Aren't

Seven thousand plus languages,
twenty million plus words,
and I'm sitting here incapable
of telling you how I feel

Twenty-seven primary emotions,
the basis for all our feelings,
and I'm sitting here incapable
of expressing what goes on inside me

So many words to describe
so few emotions,
and I am unintelligible and
nondescript

We say, "communicate."
Tell me what you're thinking, feeling.
Can't you see it's an impossibility?
And we wonder why we have so much pain

The words aren't in there.
No way to say what we need to say.
We are trapped in a lie,
a problem with no solution

John Hinton

Sharp Edges

You can't be nice anymore.
Nice has angles,
angles have sharp edges,
sharp edges cut,
and everyone is thin-skinned,
expecting to bleed

Nice is dangerous.
Hard threats in soft words,
cruel intent behind kind acts.
Nice is a silent alarm—
Warning: Deception Ahead

If we can't be nice anymore,
what are we to be?
Indifferent, withdrawn
people wearing blinders,
roaming in protective pods.
No you, just me—
castrated humanity

John Hinton

Loss

We were always living in tension;
loss will do that to a family.
The atmosphere always seemed strained.
Like that uneasy stillness before a storm,
we were afraid to speak truth lest we break the air,
as if words would unleash the torrent.
And so, to avoid the damage of a "storm"
many honest words were never spoken

He would sit in his recliner,
eyes wide open, mouth agape,
a man either gone insane or dead.
"Dad? Dad? *Dad!?*"
No response at all.
I would poke him in the chest,
pat his face as if trying to revive, sit on his lap,
scream at him, *"Dad,"* fear welling inside of me

I was just a kid—what was I supposed to do?
Fear turned to anger. What was his *problem?*
How could he *do* this to me?
He was no longer a father but a grotesque gargoyle.
In my anger, I'd give up, go away

He always came back.
Nothing was ever mentioned about his state,
he acted like nothing had ever happened,
and I, afraid of unleashing the torrent,
left many honest words never spoken.
The atmosphere was so fragile and the storm so threatening

Years have gone by, for years he's been gone,
and that damnable storm still lingers over me,
and the honest words I've never spoken I finally say today:
"Dad, in those moments, I hated you.
For those moments, I hate you still."

John Hinton

Beef on the Side of the 15

Road-tripping south,
caught by slow traffic as
far north as Douglas City,
we saw them by the thousands there
and were forced to cruise by.

They sound like people in hell, she said.

All that moronic beef, hide to hide,
pissing and shitting all over each other,
not at all knowing the reason for their existence.

If we were closer,
we could see the look in their eyes,
the reason you don't name them,
and we might relate to those beefs,
hopeless even to wonderment
at the way things are, and why.

But traffic cleared and we drove on,
probably to eat Angus later that week.

Alden Wallace Mackay

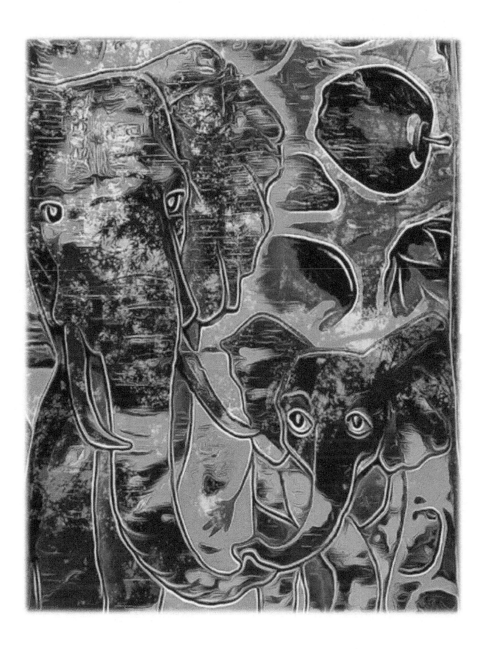

Known by Heart

for David Allen

Each day I bring the two dogs
to this park, with its tall trees,
its open spaces, its stillness,
for their outing—
                    and today
I hear something, and stand
and listen, trying to determine
the source. It is a lost music,
the flowing of distant passages
long forgotten—
                    music I studied
a lifetime ago, from childhood on,
the lessons and monthly recitals,
the endless scales and exercises,
the books with the yellow covers
that never stayed put on the piano,
that were always falling, pages
unfurling—
                    music of my early years
emerging from the battered keys
almost accidentally at first,
gradually revealing a world
of form, a place of refuge linked
indissolubly with the pressure
of my fingers, my breathing,
my early solitude—
                    music rising
from the page, from smooth drifts
of notes stretching interminably
away from me, toward some horizon
I could not imagine ever reaching
in my lifetime –
                    silhouette of tall trees
in the back country, the sycamore,
the ash, the poplar—
                    it was this music

I played for years, and came to know
by heart, but then abandoned,
eventually gave up, no longer
thought much about. The old books
lay neglected in their wooden bench.
The power of music to summon,
to come over me unexpectedly,
remained constant, but I had moved
farther from its source.
                         Such loss,
such absence, no longer matters now,
on this halcyon afternoon in October.

I have come here with the two dogs,
the Chow mix and the half Golden.
The three of us have wandered
far from our usual path—across
the field, over the concrete bridge,
and through the stand of hackberry
and the red oaks along the creek.
Here, all the leaves, blown eastward,
have finally settled. We come upon
an acre or more of russet leaves
dropped from surrounding limbs,
hushed and silent now, in no wind,
spread out before us.
                         The dogs,
unleashed, venture into this expanse,
unsure at first of their footing,
or what might wait beneath
this strange surface.
                         Slowly they begin
to discover, to their innocent joy,
that it yields, that it is evanescent,
like water, and they are invisibly
borne up. With each step, the earth
is still firm beneath their tread.

They become excited, they caper
and dance among the dry leaves,
around them everything is chance
and leafy motion, their progress
through the vast drift of lightness
made momentarily visible—
                    circles
widening on a lake where flat stones
go skipping across—
                    forgotten notes
once known by heart, returning now,
the fingers beginning to discover
the way again—
                    shadows cast
by a partial eclipse, half moons
of transitory light—
                    music comes back
whole, back from hidden recesses
in deep time—
                    the two dogs running
along the creek now, a puff of wind
rearranging, for a moment,
the scattered leaves, smoothing
the carpet again—
                    leaving no path
through the rufous drifts, as though
the dogs' crossing—their fierce joy—
never took place.
                    I am comforted.
Whether there is an ultimate ground
beneath the place where we stand,
or a path that will reveal itself,
something still remains, like music,
closer now, remotely beckoning.

                                        Jared Carter

Shades

Walk among them.
Softly, lest they scatter.
Dark-eyed juncos, hesitant,
feed on fallen seed.

Feeding voles flee
at noises imagined.
Walk among them, take notice
when the light is right,

Moments after glow,
that last wine-bodied burst,
footfalls sound no scent of dust,
only then they appear
when the light is right.

Stalk your ancient friend,
pull at his jacket sleeve,
give a gentle, weightless tug.
Unaware, caught off guard,
he disregards you
for the moment.

Bruce Ducker

Seeing Himself in A New Light

When a perceptive friend said, "I do not think you are depressed.
You do not show signs of that; instead, I think you are repressed."
Hayden was impressed. "Repression is something I can work with,"

he believed. After years of wondering about his moods
yet aware that he rose every morning, did not go back to bed
during the day, had still some appetite, and did not turn to drink
or watch more porn than he enjoyed, Hayden has wondered
what diagnosis might apply (he feels something is missing
from his life because he seldom experiences real Joy).

Now, because of the words of his friend, Hayden is on the mend:
reading charming or witty books for children and young adults,
noticing unnamed small flowers at the foot of trees when he walks
in the neighborhood, ordering a CD from Amazon
of the songs from *The Threepenny Opera* with the 1954
off-Broadway cast which included Lotte Lenya.

Hayden is on a road going up instead of down—
a path through the woods that is not much strewn
with fallen branches, offers few ruts
to avoid, is fairly devoid of undesirable detours.
Before he knows it, Hayden may whistle. Perhaps next week
he will belt out a line or two from Italian opera.

It is not that a whole new world is his. Not yet.
But after being informed he is merely repressed,
Hayden feels like a keyboard letter come unstuck.

Jonathan Bracker

An Atheist's Argument

Choir singing, strangers weeping,
eyes glued to the casket.
Pot-bellied giant shouting praises
eyes the collection basket.

"God is love.
God is life.
Man is not dead."

Fatherless Sunday schooler screams out
as his Christianity is being bled:

it gushes through the new gray suit.
pouring over nomadic relations,
kneeling in pews three deep up front,
cursing acceptance of the invitation

to comfort the grieved
and radiate some strength
till the box is firmly planted.

Then, with tearful goodbyes
and bored, relieved sighs,
they vanish with their god
to Scranton.

Mark Blickley

Stone Wishes

Her man,
a philanderer—only
sometimes does he slide
on the brass ring
of their marriage.
Husband,
like desert cactus
she can never climb,
his love's desert
drought, no oasis
in sight, where she thirsts
for what came before …

stealing hours
in the dark parlor,
breaking her fast
of silence, second chances,
and despair, swept
along by rising
winds over the bed
of sand dunes, crystal cut,
hollowed out, always
overwhelming the present
tense in memory's war
where she is bent
on small survivals.

Lee Landau

On What Level that Sick Girl

Stealing food, love a shoddy experience,
feeds her limited pleasure.
But her mother traces the missing food,
smacks her across the face
to remind her just who holds her life in their hands.
Often, she has no energy to walk to the bathroom
and wets herself. Sometimes
her mother leaves her in wet pajamas all day,
making a change
before her father returns home.
Evenings her father shows up
with a tray of betting chips
to play exactly three games of Gin Rummy.
Not much talking, but winning is fun.
She has no appetite for dinner,
the meal too heavy to swallow.
So she hides chewed steak in napkins and tissues,
waiting for her mother to remove the tray.
Bereft of family, abiding love,
she dreams of wellness, school,
other children, her sisters
who never visit—immunities a problem—school children
riddled with germs and viruses, according to her mother.
She lays in her bed long after lights out
and cries her weariness away.

Lee Landau

The Blizzard of 1950

-Eatontown, NJ

Sometimes, too many times, Mom went crazy.
Never meant for children, particularly three girls
in a low rent, attached home, three-way-shared
bedroom, and seven feet of play space in the living room.

On snowy days we played train, turned chairs
upside down and pulled blankets over their legs.
The oldest child always the conductor, and the youngest,
always the do-nothing passenger until fights
broke out, since we all wanted to be conductor,
collect tickets, announce train stops, let passengers off.

On snow days without school, fights replaced boredom.
She bundled us up in mittens, wool hats, and snow suits,
put us out, then locked the door with words like,
"Go pretend to be an icicle."

So we sat on the front step, no roof pitched
over us, minus five degrees, and waited out her mood,
no traffic in sight and toes, yes toes too numb to bend,
where snow perplexes a blue gray sky while snow
shapes us with no vocabulary left to complain.

We learned early about taking risks and its consequences,
knew not to knock or ring the bell.
Punishments worse than cold would welcome us.

Lee Landau

Shoes Bear a Familiar Design
What Changed in 1958?

Aging snows a storm
of implications—I feel alive, life made simple,
a skirt flared like a triangle and the shirt
forgotten, uninformed body parts stuck
to a shaky line with Minnie Mouse
shoes and Raggedy Ann hair.
The authentic me, the existential me.
Change fails to describe the relentless
storm, the open world earned in spite of
paying the piper. My early twenties
absorbed gravity's rockslide.
I would draw myself as a stick figure, not
too different from early
childhood renderings: Thin lips
shape the mouth downward.

This relentless storm with black and white streamers
rocking out the night in Red Bank, New Jersey.
Here my older sister broke the color line:
friends in school, but don't
socialize at parties. Don't date, don't boyfriend Negros.
Between white rock and roll, raucous joy,
Nat King Cole, and B.B. King, Motown mixed
those bodies up, some smoking
joints from the scent of it. Our lyrical
world of movement. Our twelve years
of schooling shared, friends now huddled
against her. By midnight,
Negros still traveled home, across
railroad tracks away from our white
neighborhood—driving
oh-so-slowly, avoiding
police detection and possible jail time.

Lee Landau

Raining Someplace, Maybe

That heart barely tunes up the body. I lie
on my back, show limbs askew like some floppy doll,
motionless as the eyes shed water courting its own rhythm.
No singing here, rhythm and blues floating away, tears
that launder me speechless. Singing lost to heart & mind,
sound paused for the steady beat of rappers not timed out.
Even draughts of hot coffee do not initiate heart rhythms in
this Pandemic time, all allegory wrapped around me, cause
panic from germs I cannot see that surround us all.
Life is a cheap commodity now. I hide in my apartment
where this quiet life wearies me, living inside my skull.
Bones rattle like dice in a game of chance, impossible
to win. Quarantine, Lockdown, Social Distancing, Masks turn
all into potential criminals up to some mayhem.
Do my eyes smile to invoke your trust? I suspect mid-lobe
entropy, no happy space, muscular strength is not enough
to stir any passion.

Lee Landau

Drunk Watch

Dedicated to all the kids, brothers, sisters, wives, husbands, and family members
who are on watch tonight and any night

Are you on tonight?
Yep, I am,
just like every night.
Nope it's not fun.
It's degrading and it's boring.
Not for the drunks, though.
Remember, it's their right
to drink every night
of the year
for as long as they want,
as much as they want.
Do you ever wonder
if they ever think
how it is for us?

I feel for the homeless drunks
who have no one
to watch over them,
who drink alone,
remain alone.

What do you do on your watch?
Me? I hide out.
Right after I see
the third drink downed,
that's my signal
to exit to the next room,
get outside, downstairs,
anywhere but the same room.
Drunks need to be watched from a distance.
You need to stay out of their way.

RM Yager

Marauders of the Basest Kind

At the cusp of a great week, I think
my anxiety has left me for good. I spy
its stiff, lifeless body outside my workplace,
poke it twice with a stick before I continue
my stroll down the city sidewalk, relieved.
I do not see its insidious grin as it yawns
awake behind my back

In its favorite piss-filled alley,
it produces chemical excretions
to change its own ether — clever
little fellow: just your typical,
late-blooming serial killer,
dormant for so long I'd forgotten it even existed

It marches now, triumphant,
at the head of a band, knees
high. It cackles and clangs
cymbals, gleefully pounds
on empty garbage cans
until it spies my silhouette
ahead and shimmies after me
down the cracked street, so eager
to overtake me. It craves
the warmth of its own
filth and finds a wanton
camaraderie in a putrid
swarm of flies, each party
dazzled by this disruption:
marauders of the basest kind

This newborn gang chortle raucously,
slap each other on the back, pile
on one drunken anecdote after another of how
they've managed to trip me up
yet again

Melody Wang

The Unexpected Return

An alignment of wind-swept elements
seems to alter a barred owl's song—the sharp
gasp of a minor refrain setting off a tinny
ringing in the ears of those slightly more attuned

As if finally granted permission, the starved
tide below lets out a frenzied howl
and begins to lap at pale, deformed
rocks encrusted with sea urchins

The house on the hill is unmoved. The air rustles
as something shimmies in with a ghost's dry breath,
bone chilled as the antique wines blooming with
ease in a forgotten corner of the basement cellar

Upstairs, a baby turns over in her wooden crib,
solemn eyes fixated on the thick, starless night
beyond the curtain—something crouches
in the darkness, silent and waiting

The new mother paces the room, pulls her shawl
more tightly around her, and shivers at glimpses
of her own ephemeral youth and something
else reflected in her baby's shining eyes

Melody Wang

Tucked Away in My Desk Drawer, I Find

The old shuffle that contains the first
       grainy demo he sent to me, those
       subtle bass notes flourishing
       with the first few sweet breaths
       I was able to take with this new
       yellow inhaler prescribed to me
       when that bad cough somehow
       brought back my childhood asthma.

The last oxygen meter left on the shelf
       that night we drove to CVS
       on my birthday, panicked
       that I couldn't breathe.
       I haven't used it since.

The roll-on Tahitian vanilla perfume
       I wore the first time I heard
       that one song, the lead singer's
       sultry crooning *that's alright with me*
       as if I could somehow be okay
       with this faded friendship
       I thought we'd hold onto.

The fifteen packs of birth control
       that came the day after
       I decided to stop taking them.

The flash drive that contains God
       knows what & I know so little
       still about the world and my place
       in it, and I want so much to pause
       this record before these days
       become a memory I only
       revisit when the mood strikes.

Back then, we sought out the light
we somehow recognized in each other.
Back then   it was enough.

Melody Wang

Absence, No

An author's explanation regarding the following poem is in order. *Absence, No* was originally written for two purposes. First, to honor the author's daughter and late granddaughter, Emilie Hobbs. Emilie was an aspiring research scientist when she died of sudden heart failure during an evening marathon training run at Purdue University, where she was a doctoral candidate in microbiology and chemistry. Emilie had a rare but undetected heart anomaly. The poem seeks to capture elements of the thoughts and emotions of her mother in response to her daughter's passing. Ordinary rules of punctuation regarding question marks and certain sentence arrangements are not followed in the poem in its quest to portray the interplay of cognition and emotion in a person's mind, heart, and soul. Second, the poem seeks to support the mission of the Emilie Hobbs Memorial Fund, established three years ago by her parents, which includes testing for rare heart conditions by high school and college athletic programs, the promotion and use of AED's by athletic programs, and the provision of scholarships to senior female STEM students planning to go to a four year college in Indiana. For more information, see www.running-for-emilie.org

We will always be running with Emilie.
The thoughtful emotion did not abate,
it was welcomed she said to herself.

Her searches continued their journey.
There are empty spaces in the closet.
More so on the periphery of vision.
Even in light chatter or worthy talk,
in gaps that appear in movies,
and scarily realized after long drives.

Recently, she had been reading Camus.
We will always be running with Emilie.
Is that what Camus understood,
did she find that among his words.
Who did he run for, write for,
what possibilities did he inspire
as many carried him
in the prosaic violence of any life.

We will always be running with Emilie.
Why stop. Why settle for less.
Why shorten what is best even in absence
while lifting forward with presence.

Questions asked and some answered.
She moved ahead running in the dark
to reach the light of the coming day
running with Emilie.

John I. Cardwell

For the Drag Queens on 14th Street

Outside my bar,
I've watched them
waiting for desperate
customers, sharing
the same expression.

In between episodes of
terror and boredom,
only the money is real.

Some are killed,
but the newspapers want real news,
and the cops want easier overtime.
There's no adrenaline
or fresh bank notes in the budget
for so-called freak killings.

These queens impersonate
a different sex so well
they could be retouched photographs.

But the fingerprints left are damaging,
never invisible. Each
night, life is a warped
Disneyland of
drugs, alcohol, & fear.

It's raining havoc
tonight on the disguise,
but there they are
on 14th St. selling fantasy,
yet only the money
is real ... and the
future unimaginable.

Rp Verlaine

The Ignored Promises

Like a lost bank receipt
adds up to less than
empty space,
you feel going
to work almost
sober in clothes
almost clean as
a general's hands
gesticulating orders
that mean men
will die.

Knowing only the
fatal flaws of plans
never meant to include
you.

Any more than a curtain
pulled back ever
shows you a reason
or answer, just a
tease that death
is a closer
and the good life
a rumor you no
longer care to share.

As retirement looms.

Before the
bankrupt fading light
of the moon, the mad
indifferent song of
fate, and love the lie
I've made
and left it at.

Death creeps closer,
no longer needing
the circuitous route.

It's not pity I want,
just kindness
or hope,
even if
it's as slight as a robin's
faint cry.

Before the darkness,
I want a bright fleeting light
over what's been
and will be.

One more kiss that matters.
One more perfect dance
around all I've known,
I thought precious,
and a well-said goodbye.

As death comes
from the
shadows,

I dare it closer
with a smile
to say, *okay,*

let's go.
But let me
have a final beer
first.

                    Rp Verlaine

                    100

The Slow Suicides

Find me with
their eyes of
incalculable hurt.

Their sad laughter
hollow, and their
touch always distant,

having endured pain
in ways that most
cannot fathom.

From assaults
to rape to degradation
of selling themselves

to buy heroin
and other opioids—
a too-temporary fix.

Others trespass to
a thousand deep holes
or sequester in depression.

They will find me
unable to save them,
knowing that I can't.

I give them advice
seldom listened to
as they walk toward fire,

fearless and alone,
exhausted by everything
but a vague promise

of where peace exists
in solitude deafening except
for the death bells' ring

Rp Verlaine

Old Friends

I went with a friend to a circus
where he had worked in younger days.
We had cold pop and fresh popcorn that
went down nicely on the hot evening.
After the performance,
we went back to visit
with his old friends.
The café was open for late diners,
performers too exhausted to cook.
The workday wasn't ended because
performers and animal keepers
helped lower tent beams after
removing costumes and makeup
and feeding the animals.
Everyone was occupied, for work wasn't
done until they were packed
to move to their next job.
Joyful calls rang out
as men recognized my friend,
and as they heard his familiar voice,
the elephants trumpeted
their welcome, too.

Joyce Zephyrin

Pandemic in the First Hours of Spring

Weeds and garlic push through
rotting, leafy soil in the garden,
bright green with urgency;
silhouette of a robin at pre-dawn,
caught up in the bantering chorus,
as you go off to work
in uncertainty. We at our age
just learning to be happy
at this stage of things.
What I would give,
what I would take.

Yellow Finches

Every day I am alive,
they feed
on tiny plants
going to seed or flower
that grow
between cobblestones
on my street,
then fly
to the birdbath at the edge
of the garden,
where they drink
as if
I will always care.

D.E. Laczi

The Elephant in the Room

Dark, loud, and heavy,
the elephant lay upon the room,
relinquishing to silence the stage.
Silence becoming the star of this space,
rendering assistance from only tears.
As though on que,
tears surged
from the hardest of stones
and down through mere pebbles,
incontrollable,
inconsolable,
comfortless.
Swollen, disheartened,
bloodshot traces displayed
evidence of the path of pain,
proceeding from the innermost
depths of the soul
and flooding eyes.
Gnawing pain gripped
the brokenness,
creating ceaseless
cries of anguish
and moans of misery
that violently pierced
that silent stage.
The elephant suffocated all
but silence and sorrow
while it floated upon tears,
drowning any hope for tomorrow.
Goodbye now an impassable mountain,
and comfort
an unattainable climb.
No words could be said
as the elephant floated in this gloom.

Teresa Pruitt

Ineffable

I don't remember
when you were born.

I wasn't around. I
never heard your first
cry, your first sound,
your first spoken word.
I was not your father.

But I was
always there,
somewhere in a place
we lost and never found.

These regrets scatter,
falling upon the once-warm-
hearted ground like memories
that I cannot recall. They fall
around my feet in fragments,
bits and pieces of unidentified
emotions. I saw your first step
just now imprinted, interwoven
tightly with my soul, within the crystal
patterns that now feel so much like snow.

All these moments gather
against me and lie incredibly still
as my body becomes older
and my hair turns gray. They
huddle together on this windowsill,
press against the glass of my soul in a way ineffable.

James Eric Watkins

Symbolism

I realized some years ago
that I didn't need to stand
over the burial ground of
the dead to feel close to them,

but that they exist within us,
inside every beautiful and sad
moment we shared together

and from anywhere, be it
gazing out over a field of swaying grass
or standing on a cold slab of concrete
in silence or reading elegant words from leaf.
We can be enveloped by their spirits,

knowing that their energies have always
been, neither created nor destroyed,
but perpetually existing and transforming.

And so, markers upon the earth
or urns sitting quietly upon their mantles,
ashes scattered within the wind
or carried away by rushing water
are simply (but importantly)

symbols,
calming our fear
that we may forget.

James Eric Watkins

These Hands

They look
like my father's,
scarred and spotted.

One night when we were young,
my father blew out all the lightbulbs
with a shotgun and an evil smile
until we shivered in the dark.

Alone. Quiet. Smart.

When we awoke
from our cocoons
into the bright morning light,

no one spoke,
no one looked
into anyone's eyes.

And later that same day,
I paid close attention
to the details of his hands

as the new light bulbs were passed
from mine to his, lifted up
and screwed into the sockets.

James Eric Watkins

Venus Rising

The sunset has shed blue sapphires
over the parking lot. Drinks after a movie.
It's a nice place. Civilization flies a flag
of timid complacence and neon lights.
Only a bright star rises over the dark hills.
You must feed yourself to the moon wolves
hiding in the ancient hills.
Wild bulls and storm terrors live there.

You must become skeletal. Dead but ever living.

And there is a golden lynx guarding a bow
you aim at the heart of the Milky Way

in those dark hills.

                              Diana Thoresen

Stolen Memories

I

A twelve-point buck has become a trophy
for some middle-aged guy who needs
to mount bragging rights to camouflage
his mundane life: gulping beer to numb
feelings, to forget failed dreams and
small paychecks—no consideration
for this buck's life snuffed out in an instant,
from does waiting for him with nesting fawns,
from memories of running
through the woods, of another rut season,
of finding fresh berries, crunchy
acorns, and tender leafy greens.

II

Mom closes her eyes to the world
knowing her best days are behind her:
standing tall in mini-skirts and go-go boots,
of meeting Tom Jones, slinging panties
on stage, she's missing moments
laughing with great-grandchildren, holding
her newest great-great, forgetting loved ones
by the day, and her mind can't tell her why.
She can't know the freedom of running,
now confined to a wheelchair. She feels
a burden to her family, and heaven knows
she should've eaten more tomatoes, walnuts,
blueberries, and fresh leafy greens.

Lylanne Musselman

Let There Be Light

God said, "Let there be light,"
and light undulated over the formless stuff
of the ground and in the skies
to the extent of God's endless imagination.
God laughed and the waves of God's laughter
undulated as far and as completely as the light.
"This is good," God said.

Galileo said, "The earth revolves around the sun."
The Inquisitors said that was heresy.
"You have made liars of Joshua, Moses, and the Bishops at Trent."
Galileo, his telescope in hand, said, "E pur si muove."
God said, "Non va bene, Monsignori.
You want stasis, but I set all in motion."

Maxwell said, "Electrical fields generate magnetic fields
that generate electrical fields,
which in turn generate magnetic fields,
and they roll on together
througout God's endless expanse
like puppies chasing each other in delight."
God said, "Jolly good, James.
You grasped the joy of it."

John D. Groppe

Natural Selection

A one-legged sandpiper hunches and hops,
hunches and hops. She needs to compete
for a promising place in the tumbling surf,
letting the waves carry food to her since
she is no longer able to run for it.
I believe she expected to die—
the amputation making her solitary—
but appetite drove her to try.

Muscles propel her into a wave.
Her neck has grown supple from stretching,
her eye has grown sharper from foraging,
her mind made agile in the face of survival.

She considers each move in careful detail,
then hunches and hops to retrieve the next meal.

Ann Borger

Sonatina

My newlywed parents played duets,
her piano accompanying his violin.
In World War II, his ear and hands
transcribed Morse code. At home,
Mom and I listened to the radio:
music, interrupted by commercials,
followed by news. "Somewhere
in the Pacific" was the Sixth Fleet.
When Dad came home, his fingers
knew a different tune. The radio—
old vacuum tubes—stopped working.
I learned piano, ever frustrated by
the difference between what I played
and the way I intended it.

Ann Borger

Pointing Fingers at Extinction

"Hey look, kids! There goes a lightning bug!"
I shouted from across the yard.
"What? Where?" they asked, perking up from their devices.

I casually pointed across the yard
with eyebrows lifted,
encouraging them to venture on towards the garden behind the shed.

They both went back to gaming.

Slowly, I sunk back into the hot tub,
somewhat disappointed by their lack of interest.
"Maybe that's my fault," I thought to myself.
"Maybe I should be more engaging and lead them on the hunt."

Sipping on a cold beer,
my pride returned as I overlooked this season's efforts
in grooming a perfectly manicured lawn.
"Here's to the last American lightning bug,"
I mumbled to Sonia, lifting my drink to cheer its dying efforts.
It glowed one last time,
and then faded away into the dark memory of night.

"When we were kids,
we used to smash their guts in the streets,
spelling out our names in endless neon slime.
This neighborhood was rich with them when we were younger."

I knew she couldn't hear me with her head halfway underwater,
gazing up at the sky.

"I wonder where they've all flown to … where they all went.
A mass migration to Japan's Grave of Fireflies?
Perhaps extermination?
I'm sure it's from the neighboring farmer's pesticides.
There's no way us kids could've killed them all."

Levi Rinker

Stocking Up

My husband and I make salsa,
use homegrown tomatoes,
peppers, onions, cilantro,
boil full jars for fifteen minutes.
I lug them down to the cellar,
line them up with the others—
twenty-one this year—
too many for the two of us.

I think of my dad when
Mom fell to the floor
with her final stroke,
cans of formula for her feeding tube
stacked on shelves in the closet.

I don't know what he did with them.
What would I do with jars of salsa
if suddenly left alone?

Love pushes us forward.
We fill baskets with food for tomorrow,
refuse to believe there is an end.

Jan cister

New Place

Unpacking the last box, I happen on this
picture of him, a stranger I once lived with
month-to-month while I looked for something

cheaper. He lost his arm at seven when
his brother made him climb a telephone pole
and touch the live wire. The fall should've

killed me, he said, but I landed in a garden bed
our neighbor had recently turned. I had to relearn
how to write, how to draw, how to throw a ball.

Late at night, we'd talk about our brothers,
how hard it was to forgive. He loved bragging
about the amount he could handle: make a call,

pound a burger, and drive stick shift all at once.
When we juggled clubs, he'd tease me for using two
hands but we both knew we needed three

to make the pattern work. I don't know where
he is now, or what he does, or if he's in touch
with his brother. In the photograph he's jammed

himself into the small gap between the mirror
and clawfoot tub. Eyes shut, smirking, he lifts
his palm into the air which perfectly doubles

its reflection so he looks like a priest offering
benediction. I don't remember taking it,
but someone did, and I was the only one there.

Anders Carlson-Wee

The Mattress

No car to drive to the dump and too embarrassed
to borrow one, you scrape the black mold
off the underside as best you can, muscle it
onto your shoulder. Spores multiplied to the size
of you, the rough shape, born night after night
by the heat of your sleep. So late you lurch
down Hennepin without notice. Turning
at Taylor, you pause between streetlights, crease
the mattress in half and squat on the fold
so you won't have to face it. You're almost
to the bridge when a cop's spotlight throws
the awful bulk of your shadow onto concrete.
Where you going with that thing?
You make up a story. Is it yours? You admit it is.
Not your best look, Junior. Yes, you play along,
I should change. The cruiser turns down 8th,
and a moment later a coal train rattles under
the bridge on its way out of the country. You brace
the mattress on the guardrail and pivot
the weight, torquing it down through the dark
where it lands on the black coal and pulls
north like shame itself on a conveyer belt,
the mold gazing up at you like the aborted face
of what, all by yourself, you have made.

Anders Carlson-Wee

Footprint

Throw away eggs, and I make
breakfast; plastic, and I weave

rugs; duct tape, and I reinforce
a chair leg; milk cartons

and I plant seeds, start
a nursery. Your torn jacket

gets hemmed. Busted shades
get jimmyrigged. Throw away

Tidy Cat buckets, and I add
hardware, convert them to rain-

proof panniers. Your mail,
and I read it. Your pencils,

and I write. Throw away
hundreds of pounds of tea,

and I draw baths thickened
with hundreds of bags

of chamomile. Bent nails
straighten. Warped wood warps

back. Throw away frames,
and I frame whatever else

you threw away, hang it
on my wall like a portrait.

                            Anders Carlson-Wee

Hearing the News

Hearing the news of the latest climate report—
the "Code Red for Humanity"—I am not surprised.
The world's ablaze
and drowning,
confirming years of predictions.

Yet my heart laments
and legs are leaden.
Familiar sensations,
the language my body spoke
during the years of David's decline.

Then, too, I'd done the research
and knew what was coming,
though with each loss
my heart winced at evidence
that despite all the doctors, therapists, pills, prayers,
and denial,
the disease was gaining.

With today's climate news,
I again face my impotence.
I don't know how to persuade
the world's top polluters to care.
I don't know how to convince those in denial
that this is real and advancing.

What I do know
is how to cherish the time I have
with a beloved whose future is uncertain.

I know how to revel
in the preciousness of a life
on the verge of unraveling.

So I savor more deeply now
the brush of midnight breeze on my skin
at the end of another blistering day.

I praise birds that still sing at dawn,
crickets that still chant at night.

I exhale at the sight of fireflies
and the curve of new moon's sliver at twilight.

I smile at cloud shapes
while floating on my back
in the middle of a lake that I love.

But today, I meet myself weeping
on my yoga mat
as I sometimes did in the last year
of his life.

Rosanne Megenity Peters

The Elephant in the Room

Contrary to what has been said, they do talk about me—a lot. Even the couch complains when I sit on it. Other topics occasionally dominate the conversation, but sooner or later, it always comes back to me. They deny it, but their *voce* is not as *sotto* as they like to think. When the chain on my foot clanks too loudly, I read their lips. At first it was harmless jokes, calling me Little Peanut, their sentient vacuum cleaner, living shower head—that kind of thing. But all that changed when I crushed the family dog underfoot. They told each other it was an accident, but I could see they had their doubts. Now they worry I've grown too much. They don't consider that maybe the room is getting smaller. The renovations, which took longer than expected (as expected), were supposed to make everything airier, but no sooner had the floor plan opened than they began filling it with more stuff. No one stopped to consider how a piano smiling in the corner might make me feel. They just keep chattering on about where I came from, what I'm doing here, how long I'm going to stay, why I smell like that, etc. Sometimes late at night, their voices drift up to the ceiling and hover there in a noisy little cloud. It reminds me of the monkeys and that makes me sad.

Peter Anderson

Animosity

We scattered the shattered remains across our field of vision, hoping they would bear fruit when the season turned. We forgot we'd done it until shards poking out from the earth cut the soles of our feet, branding our steps. We watched the green exclamation marks of stems grow burdened with buds and assume the posture of question marks. When they flowered, passing pedestrians stopped to breathe the fragrance. Even the allergic paused to admire the delicate hues. We smiled red-eyed before limping back into our house and breaking everything in sight.

Peter Anderson

Humanity

We get up and read the news. In the evening, we watch viral videos. Animals laughing at our magic tricks. We have a friend who handles snakes and likes to say people are a virus on the earth. He actually says cancer, but virus sounds timelier. In this time of. What does he make of what we're going through? In the beginning days, we thought it'd bring us closer, humble us, enlarge our sense of who we are. Not make us smaller, more ill at ease in this world. Rilke said that, or something like it. Nothing original. All these clichés, like spring-loaded traps buried in the forest floor. We come here to study nature, when suddenly we find ourselves upended, suspended by a foot from a tree. Taken from our family, our loved ones, our natural habitat, caged and studied to see what makes us different, what makes us similar. By the time we're released back into the wild, we've grown fond of our captors. We stop to hug them. Maybe they've saved us from ourselves. More research is needed.

Peter Anderson

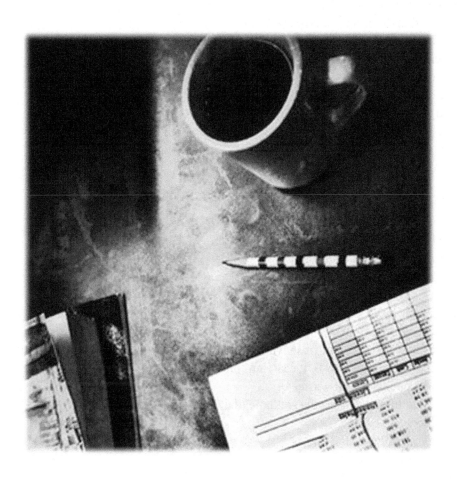

Millenium

It started with hierarchy:
our first ancestors picked
the one most likely to kill
those who'd strayed too far
and let him decide how all of us would live.
After a few Ice Ages, we
realized there was even more stuff we
could not control.
Then came the wheel,
the cave,
the cities,
and suddenly there were so many of us,
our problems went up exponentially.
Then government,
drinking water, sewers,
and protecting ourselves from the kin
of those we'd killed long ago
when they encroached on our turf.
And then poets
who railed against everything
because folks liked the sound of that,
both sides suspecting
disorder was keeping up
with progress.
And for every gallon of fresh water
we cupped from the well, the stream, the lake,
another bucket of our waste
appeared in the aquifer, the sinkhole, the fen.
The poets loved this,
the maidens loved the poets,
and their children became civil engineers
who built sewage treatment plants and reverse osmosis,
and taxed the populace
who drove them over the mountains
across the Bosporus and Dardanelles,
past the kingdoms of Kublai Khan
where they studied catapults and trigonometry

Paul Smith

Elephants

Elephants mourn their dead
for several days,
placing branches over the carcass
and, in some cases,
taking the tusks somewhere else to bury them.
Giraffes mourn, too,
congregating in a tower,
passing by their loved one,
reaching down with their long necks
and touching the body,
some bending their knees
to get the whole body even lower
in an act of reverence
that approximates genuflecting
before they disperse.
We sometimes mourn our dead
by going to the zoo,
finding a familiar wooden bench
we sat on a year ago,
a bench that comforts an arthritic hip,
and contemplating
how long are those tusks,
how long the giraffes' necks are,
and do they know they're in a zoo?
Food is brought to them.
They don't even have to stretch
to get those topmost leaves
of the nearby trees.
How long do they live?
Do they contemplate the afterlife,
or does the drive to forage
keep them going till the end?
Maybe it's like seeing a far-off acacia tree,
its limbs all melancholy and drooping,
trekking their way to reach its succulent leaves,
a feast they somehow know
they will never get to.

Paul Smith

127

My Mother's Elephant

I remember well that little bone china elephant
that sat on my mother's vanity,
small and white, its trunk turned in and eyes closed.

It was more than an ornament—
it was a key to imagination and creativity.

I remember the days it roamed the African safari
and locked its trunk and tail with others,
making a long link that never ended, spanning the Serengeti.

The time it watched that old movie with me
and learned to stretch out its ears and fly around the room.

Then there was the journey to India
where it bore a large golden and jewel covered howdah,
carrying the Maharaja in a grand parade
where the crowd tossed roses and bowed to beauty.

Yes, I remember those adventures well,
but perhaps the most incredible tales of this elephant are yet to be told.
The stories my child will envision as they play with it.
Awaking the elephant from its long slumber
as it sat atop my dresser,
waiting to roam the jungle or escape from the circus.
I will wait to see all that this elephant will never forget.

W.B. Cornwell

Becoming Cyclonic

Enveloped in unbreakable Duplo
behind toy telephones with rotary dials,
there's a tiny examination room
where I find myself sitting like a giant pebble,
or a pebble which finds itself sitting like me.

My significant other speaks.
We discover the existence of a bright little pill
which sands edges off the gloom.

A neurotypical-fly-on-the-wall-me
might appreciate the moment,
sensing change,
a balm of fresh linen
billowing up and over tired bodies.

But going dark in pharmaco-survival mode
is dwelling under horse blinkers;
the full spectrum dances out of view,
feelings tuck themselves into crescents.

Like a kid in a trolley,
I slip down supermarket aisles
spewing medicated insights,
unsure which of my thoughts I've voiced.
Some part of me rants
about why anyone really bothers
with different flavors of ice cream,
all protons, neutrons, and electrons
in the end.

I'm trying, you see, but look
how easy it is when the wind shifts
to completely lose a scent.

Will Griffith

129

Homecoming

Welcome home, son,
reads the memo I decode
from cruciform wings,
and a thorax
death exposed.

A wanderer's undignified end
on a windowsill,
subordinate
even to jaundiced blinds.

The rest of the message
doesn't quite get through,
like mumbles from an answerphone
heard only once.

Still, here's a morning signal
just filtering in:
something about childhood dreams
exiled to who knows where.
Boneless. Grounded.

I know you are not my father,
the terminus of all journeys,
waiting in an empty house for a lost son.
Take my woolen jumpers,
next your larvae in them,
watch them gorge unmolested
until they fly.

In a sort of patchy covenant,
we will welcome all things home.

                              Will Griffith

Childhood Memories: The Elephant in the Room

A dubbed black and white film that has no sound.
Her background is in her foreground,
spinning around.
She tries desperately to make sense of past events.
Each step near, she feels more fear, more rigid, more tense.
Tries to relive each scene, to understand what they mean,
to apply reason where none exists.
Memories upsetting, they still cause pain.
A wheel spinning, revolving, again and again.
Trying to touch a hand in a swirling mist,
she looks for peace but only sees war.
Only if her search can cease
will she find the right door
that will stop the sliding around, feeling out of control.
Stroke the head of a restless soul,
take her away from the abyss, the edge, the border,
to assess reality of the present,
restore calm and order,
to know herself, who she is, what life happens for.
She needs to learn,
to close the door.

Daniel Godward

Lies

The elephant at family gatherings,
even before my birth, was our story,
or lack of one. Evasive answers.
Warnings. Birth roster missing.
Fodder for an active imagination.
Stories from Aunt Rose.
Was Grandfather really a deserter
from the Prussian Army? Did he smuggle
across the mountains, running in stocking feet
from the Red Army? White Russian
Was all we knew. I was driven for more.

They were known as Miller. Seven children
growing up as Miller, never asking why
the family Bible held the name Krinke.
A letter found, translated from Old Script,
half Russian, half German,
verified Polish Corridor roots.
Time on my hands in a pandemic year
led me to drop the global chase
for now. One call took me back to an 1890s
fragile leather binder placed in my hands.

I found my family. Not Miller—Krinke.
All names from an old country.
And more. My Grandfather's father
no longer a secret. Two babies lost
to oblivion, graveyard destroyed
and now a parking lot. No records.

His unmarked grave is beside the park,
alone with the secrets and lies.
We are Krinke. Not Miller.
They lied to everyone
except God.

KJ Carter

Firegirl

Crayons fall
from her small hands
as she shoots through the house
screaming
"Fire!"

She stomps frantically
at the flames
chasing her feet
while her mom remains head-down,
scrubbing stubborn stains
on the white enamel of the kitchen sink.

Smoke rising up her nose,
she cries with her burnt voice
as her father sits,
weary,
annexed to the couch,
holding the tumor in his head.

Her brother and sister
glance at her
over their shoulders
as they slowly walk away,
immune to the heat from years
of repeated exposure.

Desperate
to turn their gaze
away from their flailing souls
towards her own,
she strikes a match
and shakily sets afire
her flowery cotton dress.

Kim Watanabe

Wind Chimes on a Still Day

Resting in the hand-me-down oak chair
inherited from a lost branch
our tree sacrificed in decades past,
I ponder the weather of the times
& that of this outside world.

It's still, so much that you can cut
particles hanging around &
hear them fall in their dying descent.

Is Earth continuing its revolution
around our massive solar star,
or am I delusional in my state?

Sometimes, it appears
I am alone,
but the resounding ring
from chimes outside
without any wind
signals otherwise.

Tin Heerdink

David Allen was born in the South and raised on Long Island. He is a retired journalist with almost four decades on newspapers in New York,  Virginia, and Indiana, and in the Far East, he spent nineteen years reporting for *Stars and Stripes,* the newspaper for the U.S. military community overseas. He is a member of the Last Stanza Poetry Association and the Poetry Society of Indiana, where he served as vice president and contest director. He is also the host of open mic poetry nights in Anderson, IN. David has been published in numerous poetry journals and anthologies and has published four books of poetry, *The Story So Far, (more), Type Dancing,* and *Deadlines Amuse Me.* davidallenpoet.net.

Peter Anderson was born and raised in the suburbs of Detroit and now lives in Vancouver, Canada. His recent work has appeared or is forthcoming in *Unbroken, Sublunary Review, Flora Fiction Literary Magazine, Better Than Starbucks, MoonPark Review, Rat's Ass Review,* and the *American Journal of Poetry.* His plays are available online at the Canadian Play Outlet.

Mahasweta Baxipatra lives and teaches in Bloomington, Indiana. Baxipatra writes poems and nonfictional prose, and translates fiction from various Indian languages to English. She can be reached at mahabax@gmail.com

Delilah Bleu is a pseudonym for a domestic violence survivor. She began writing of her experiences during the pandemic, as instances of such abuse—and her concern for those involved—have risen dramatically. She chooses not to be visible in order to preserve her safety.

Mark Blickley grew up within walking distance of the Bronx Zoo is a proud member of the Dramatists Guild and PEN American Center. His videos, *Speaking in Bootongue* and *Widow's Peek: The Kiss of Death,* represented the United States in the 2020 year-long international world tour of *Time Is Love: Universal Feelings: Myths & Conjunctions,* organized by esteemed African curator, Kisito Assangni.

Kimberly Bolton is a folklore poet who has written over five hundred poems. She was one of forty-three poets worldwide to be published in

Poetry Super Highway *Yom Hashoah* issue for spring 2019. Several of her poems have been performed on stage, including her narrative poem "The Tale of Mercy Periwinkle." Her poetry has been published on the Medusa's Kitchen Poetry website and *Last Stanza Poetry Journal.* She has written two books of folklore poetry, *Folk* and *Tales from Grindstone Creek.* She is currently working on her third book, *Trees & Broomsticks,* due out next year. She currently lives in Jefferson City, Missouri near her beloved Missouri River.

Ann Borger is a retired computer systems analyst and choral musician as well as an award-winning poet. She began writing and publishing poems in midlife. She and her husband have lived in the Indianapolis area since 2010.

Jonathan Bracker's poems have appeared in *Last Stanza Poetry Journal, The Midwest Quarterly, The New Yorker, Poetry Northwest, Southern Poetry Review,* and other periodicals, and in eight collections, the latest of which, from Seven Kitchens Press, is *Attending Junior High.* Bracker is the editor of *Bright Cages: Selected Poems of Christopher Morley*, co-author with Mark I. Wallach of *Christopher Morley,* and editor of *A Little Patch of Shepherd's Thyme: Prose Passages of Thomas Hardy Arranged as Verse.*

Michael Brockley is a retired school psychologist who lives in Muncie, Indiana where he is looking for a dog to adopt. His poems have appeared in *Global Poemic, Woolgathering Review,* and *Fatal Flaw.* Poems are forthcoming in *Flying Island* and *The Parliament Literary Magazine.*

Michael H. Brownstein has been widely published throughout the small and literary presses. His work has appeared in *The Café Review, American Letters and Commentary, Skidrow Penthouse, Xavier Review, Hotel Amerika, Free Lunch, Meridian Anthology of Contemporary Poetry, The Pacific Review, Poetrysuperhighway.com* and others. In addition, he has nine poetry chapbooks including *The Shooting Gallery* (Samidat Press, 1987), *Poems from the Body Bag* (Ommation Press, 1988), *A Period of Trees* (Snark Press, 2004), *What Stone Is* (Fractal Edge Press,

2005), *I Was a Teacher Once* (Ten Page Press, 2011) and *Firestorm: A Rendering of Torah* (Camel Saloon Press, 2012). His latest volumes of poetry, *A Slipknot to Somewhere Else* (2018) and *How Do We Create Love?* (2019), were recently released (Cholla Needles Press).

John Cardwell began writing poetry, short stories, and essays in 2009 and continues to do so today. He was born and grew up on a working farm in Tipton County, Indiana, and presently owns and manages that farm with his wife, Nancy Griffin. They have three children and several grand and great grandchildren. John studied at the Indiana University campuses in Kokomo and Bloomington and earned degrees through the IU School of Education. He had a distinguished career as an educator, public policy advocate, and non-profit CEO, including postings with the Nigerian ministry of education.

Anders Carlson-Wee is the author of *The Low Passions* (W.W. Norton, 2019), a New York Public Library Book Group Selection. His work has appeared in *The Paris Review, BuzzFeed, Ploughshares, Virginia Quarterly Review, New England Review, Oxford American*, and many other publications. His chapbook, *Dynamite*, won the Frost Place Chapbook Prize. The recipient of fellowships from the National Endowment for the Arts, Poets & Writers, Bread Loaf, Sewanee, and the Napa Valley Writers' Conference, he is the winner of the 2017 Poetry International Prize. Anders holds an MFA from Vanderbilt University and is represented by Massie & McQuilkin Literary Agents.

Dan Carpenter is a poet, fiction writer, freelance journalist, and former Indianapolis Star columnist. He has published poems and stories in many journals and is the author of two collections of poems, *More Than I Could See* (Restoration Press) and *The Art He'd Sell for Love* (Cherry Grove Collections).

Jared Carter's seventh collection of poems, *The Land Itself*, is from Monongahela Books in West Virginia. He lives in Indianapolis.

Kathy Jo (KJ) Carter, Urban Dirt Devil, is Indiana to the core, descended from Welsh farmers and Russian/Prussian ethnicity. Retired nurse, musician, and great grandmother, this mystery buff found a niche in poetry and prose. Who knew? Published in *Indiana Voice Journal, Poets of Madison County, Ink to Paper,* and *Last Stanza* Journals.

Mystery in the works! She is a member of Last Stanza Poetry Association.

Alys Caviness-Gober is an anthropologist, artist, and writer. Despite lifelong disabilities, Alys perseveres with art and nonprofit volunteering. She comes late to the life of a professional artist; after  receiving her MA in Anthropology, Alys taught Anthropology and Women's Studies at the collegiate level for several years and was a PhD candidate in Applied Linguistics until her disabilities worsened. Alys serves on the Noblesville Cultural Arts Council and is active in the local arts scene. She is the co-founder of NICE (Noblesville Interdisciplinary Creativity Expo); in 2018 NICE received an Indiana Humanities project grant. In November of 2014, she founded Logan Street Sanctuary, Inc. (LSS), an all-volunteer 501(c)(3) arts organization providing the community with diverse arts projects and programming. In July 2019, LSS rebranded as Community • Education • Arts, Inc. (CEArts), continuing many of LSS' annual place-making projects and expanding with digital content. Alys is editor of CEArts' annual submissions-driven anthology, *The Polk Street Review,* Alys' artwork, photographs, and poetry have received national and international recognition.

Jan Chronister lives in Maple, Wisconsin. She has retired from teaching writing and now tends her gardens and verses. She served for six years as president of the Wisconsin Fellowship of Poets. Jan is the author of six collections of poetry. janchronisterpoetry.wordpress.com

W.B. Cornwell is an award-winning poet, novelist, genealogy blogger,  and half of the writing team known as Storm Sandlin. Since 2014, he has been published in over a dozen books. He is a member of Last Stanza Poetry Association. In 2016, Ben and his cousin A.N. Williams organized the campaign for Elwood, Indiana's Poetry Month. He is a featured writer for Goodkin.org and is currently working on a slew of writing projects, including various charity publications, co-authorships, and screenplays.

Mary Couch, an Administrative Assistant for Taylored Systems, Inc. a technology company in Noblesville, learned the art of poetry from her mother, and two grandmothers who were storytellers and artists. She enjoys writing poems showing  her Celtic heritage by revealing the spirits that live in nature and the oneness of the universe. Her poems have been published in a variety of venues including *Poetic Nature in the Hoosierland, Twin Poetry, An Evening with the Street Review, Encore, and* Muses: Art & Writing Muse, Polk Pegasus. She is a published author on Amazon with two books: *Hoosier Haiku: Poetic Snippets from the Heartland and Hoosier WordArt: Communing with the Chippewa.* She and her mother also published a chapbook called *Two Views,* and they were both featured in *Poetry and Paint,* a book collaboration with several poets and artists. She is a past Premier Poet for the Poetry Society of Indiana.

Bruce Ducker's numerous poems and stories have been published in leading journals, including in *The New Republic; the Yale, Southern, Sewanee, Literary, American Literary, Missouri,* and *Hudson Reviews; Shenandoah; Commonweal; the New York Quarterly; the PEN/America Journal;* and *Poetry Magazine.* The prize-winning author of eight novels and a book of short fictions, he lives in Colorado.

Daniel Godward was born in Limehouse, East London, to a poor working-class family. He enjoys reading and began writing poetry from an early age, inspired by the nonsense verse of Edward Lear and Lewis Carroll. He then turned a part-time acting job into a career, following his passion. He has had small roles in feature films and lead roles in small films. He has always written poetry in his spare time and now has a Facebook page (Danny Godward Poetry) devoted to his writing. Daniel is the author of *The Ant and the Elephant* and *The Journey.* He and his loving wife live in Kent, SE England, and they have three grown children all living abroad.

James Green is a retired university professor and administrator. He has published four chapbooks of poetry and a fifth, titled *Ode to El Camino de Santiago and Other Poems of Journey*, is forthcoming from Finishing Line Press. His individual poems have appeared in literary journals in

Ireland, the UK, and the USA. His website can be found at www.jamesgreenpoetry.net

Will Griffith is a poet, teacher, and jazz aficionado. His favorite pastime is learning new instruments and attempting to play the blues on them. He has work forthcoming in *Sledgehammer Lit, Blue Moon Rising, Amethyst Review, The Chamber Mag,* and *Reach Poetry* (Indigo Dreams). He sends suspect verses into the Twittersphere @bunglerbill

 **John D. Groppe**, Professor Emeritus at Saint Joseph's College, Rensselaer, IN, has published in *Tipton Poetry Journal, Flying Island, From the Edge of the Prairie, Christianity Today, The National Catholic Reporter,* and other journals. His poem "A Prophet Came to Town" was nominated for a Pushcart Prize (2013). His poem "Sudden Death" won honorable mention in Embers poetry contest (1984). His poetry collection *The Raid of the Grackles and Other Poems* (Iroquois River Press) was published in 2016. He is listed on the Indiana Bicentennial Literary Map 200 Years: 200 Writers.

Gary D. Grossman is a Professor of Animal Ecology at the University of Georgia and has been writing poetry for over twenty-five years. His published work can be found in various reviews including: *The Acorn, Athens Parent Magazine, Blood and Fire Review, Cotton Gin, Feh, Lilliput Review, Midwestern Poetry Review, Old Red Kimono, Pearl, Poetry Motel, Night Roses, Truck,* and *Verse-Virtual.* His writing credits include 140+ scientific papers and ten years as a columnist for *American Angler Magazine.* In addition to poetry, he has a chapbook manuscript with a publisher and a manuscript of a graphic fictional memoir.

Chris Hasara is a part-time poet and father of four from Northwest Indiana. He has been fascinated by tales of the weird (Poe, Bradbury, King) from an early age. Time spent farming and gardening has made him suspicious of plants.

Tim Heerdink is the author of *Somniloquy & Trauma in the Knottseau Well*, *The Human Remains*, *Red Flag and Other Poems*, *Razed Monuments*, *Checking Tickets on Oumaumua*, *Sailing the Edge of Time*, *I Hear a Siren's Call*, *Ghost Map*, *A Cacophony of Birds in the House of Dread*, *Tabletop Anxieties & Sweet Decay* (with Tony Brewer) and short stories "The Tithing of Man" and "HEA-VEN2." His poems appear in various journals and anthologies. He is the President of Midwest Writers Guild of Evansville, Indiana.

Mark Henderson is an associate professor of English at Tuskegee University. He earned his Ph. D. at Auburn University with concentrations in American literature and psychoanalytic theory. He has poems published or forthcoming in *Cozy Cat Press*, *From Whispers to Roars*, *Defenestrationism.net*, *Bombfire*, *Former People*, *Neologism*, *Broad River Review*, *Rune Bear*, *Flora Fiction*, *Flare*, *Visitant*, *Blood Tree Literature*, and *The Closed Eye Open*. He was born and raised in Monroe, Louisiana, and currently resides in Auburn, Alabama.

John R. Hinton is an Indiana poet and writer. His writing is inspired by our daily human interactions and the accompanying emotions: love, hate,  indifference, passion. His words explore who we are, how we behave. Sometimes eloquent, other times gritty, these words seek to reveal the joy and pain of living this beautiful human existence. He is the author of two poetry collections: *Blackbird Songs* and *Held.* John is the Vice President of the Poetry Society of Indiana and a member of Last Stanza Poetry Association.

Peter Huggins is the author of seven books of poems, including the forthcoming *Small Mercies. Audubon's Engraver* and *South* were shortlisted for  the International Rubery Book Award. He has also published three books of fiction for children. *Trosclair and the Alligator* appeared on the PBS show *Between the Lions*. A recipient of a Literature Fellowship in Poetry from the Alabama State Council on the Arts, he taught for thirty-one years in the English Department at Auburn University.

David James' sixth book is *Wiping Stars from Your Sleeves* from Shanti Arts Press, due out in the fall of 2021. He teaches writing at Oakland Community College in Michigan.

Marc Janssen lives in a house with a wife who likes him and a cat who loathes him. Regardless of that turmoil, his poetry can be found  scattered around the world in places like *Penumbra, Slant, Cirque Journal, Off the Coast* and *Poetry Salzburg*. Janssen also coordinates the Salem Poetry Project, a weekly reading, the annual Salem Poetry Festival, and was a 2020 nominee for Oregon Poet Laureate.

Lorraine Jeffery delights in her closeup view of the Utah mountains after spending years managing public libraries. She has won poetry prizes in state and national contests and published over one hundred poems in various journals and anthologies, including *Clockhouse, Kindred, Calliope, Canary, Ibbetson Street, Rockhurst Review, Naugatuck River Review, Orchard Press, Two Hawks, Halcyon, Healing Muse, Regal Publishing and Bacopa Press.*

Michael Lee Johnson lived in Canada during the Vietnam era and is a  dual citizen of the United States and Canada. Today he is a poet, freelance writer, amateur photographer, and small business owner in Itasca, Illinois. Mr. Johnson is published in more than 2033 new publications. His poems have appeared in fourty-two countries; he edits and publishes ten poetry sites. He is the administrator of six Facebook poetry groups; he has several new poetry chapbooks coming out soon. He has over 533 published poems to date. He has been published in 42 countries and was nominated for two Pushcart Prize awards and five Best of the Net nominations. 233 poetry videos are now on YouTube.

LeAnn Jones is a retired social worker who enjoys reading and writing poetry. She has four granddaughters who take up her time and devotion. She likes to travel, enjoys any kind of art, dances, and practices yoga. LeAnn is a member of Last Stanza Poetry Association.

Jenny Kalahar is the editor and publisher of *Last Stanza Poetry Journal.* She is the founding leader of Last Stanza Poetry Association in Elwood, Indiana, now in its tenth year. Jenny and

her husband, poet Patrick, are used and rare booksellers. She was the humor columnist for *Tails Magazine* for several years and the treasurer for Poetry Society of Indiana. She is the author of fourteen books. Twice nominated for a Pushcart Prize, her poems have been published in *Tipton Poetry Journal, Indiana Voice Journal, Trillium, Polk Street Review, Flying Island,* and in several anthologies and newspapers. Her works can be found on poemhunter.com and *INverse,* Indiana's poetry archive. She and Patrick previously owned bookshops in Michigan and Ohio. Through her publishing house, Stackfreed Press, she has published books for numerous authors from the US and UK. laststanza@outlook.com

Patrick Kalahar is a used and rare bookseller with his wife, Jenny, and a book conservationist. He is a veteran, world traveler, avid reader, and book collector. He is a member of Last Stanza

Poetry Association. His poems have been published in *Tipton Poetry Journal, Flying Island, Rail Lines, The Moon and Humans, Polk Street Review, Northwest Indiana Literary Journal,* and *A Disconsolate Planet.* Patrick can be seen as an interviewee in the Emmy-winning documentary *James Whitcomb Riley: Hoosier Poet,* and he gives costumed and scholarly readings as Edgar Allan Poe.

Norbert Krapf, former Indiana Poet Laureate, is a native of Jasper who has published fourteen collections, the latest of which are *Indiana Hill Country Poems* and *Southwest by Midwest.* His *Homecomings* memoir,

which covers the fifty years of his writing and publishing life, will be released next year. He has edited, translated, and written a number of books about his German roots, including *Finding the Grain: Pioneer German Germans and Letters, Beneath the Cherry Sapling: Legends from Franconia, Shadows on the Sundial: Early Poems of Rainer Maria Rilke,* and *Blue-Eyed Grass: Poems of Germany.* His *Looking for God's Country* includes poems inspired by photos of Franconia by Andreas Riedel, whose photos are also included in a collection about Norbert's grandson, *The Return of Sunshine.* Poetry on Brick Street released his podcast with Helmut Haberkamm on dialect poetry (and plays) in their Off the Bricks series.

D.E. Laczi began writing in the early 1980s. She has had publications in a number of journals and magazines, such as *Tears in the Fence, The Louisville Review, Snowy Egret, The Sow's Ear Poetry Review,* and *The Journal of Kentucky Studies,* among others.

Lee Landau produced her first poem at twelve years old, and continues to write poetry, flash fiction and short fiction. Her poems have been published in *Wisconsin Review, Cathexis Northwest, New Millennium Writings,* and *Reed Magazine,* among many others. She has workshopped with Billy Collins, Dara Weir, Tom Lux, Sharon Olds, and Jude Nutter. Lee is a recent transplant from Minnesota to the Gulf shore of Florida where she retired. She was a finalist in four poetry contests and won Honorable Mention in two others.

Alden Wallace Mackay has appeared in numerous literary magazines across Canada and the US, including *Eunoia Review, Poetica Review,* and *Cloud Carnival.* He is the author of *Endless Nights,* his debut collection. Read more at aldenwallacemackay.com

Lylanne Musselman is an award-winning poet, playwright, and visual artist, living in Indiana. Her work has appeared in *Pank, The New Verse*  *News, Rose Quartz Magazine,* and *The Ekphrastic Review,* among others. Recently, one of her poems was selected as the featured poem in *Tipton Poetry Journal,* Issue # 48 Spring 2021. Musselman's work has appeared in many anthologies, including *The Indianapolis Anthology* (Belt Publishing, 2021). She is the author of six chapbooks, including *Paparazzi for the Birds* (Red Mare 16, 2018) and is the author of the full-length poetry collection, *It's Not Love, Unfortunately* (Chatter House Press, 2018). Musselman is currently working on several chapbooks and a new manuscript.

Robert Okaji served without distinction in the U.S. Navy, and once won a goat-catching contest. The author of multiple chapbooks, his poetry has appeared in *Book of Matches, Taos Journal of International Poetry & Art, Buddhist Poetry Review,* and elsewhere.

Rosanne Megenity Peters lives in Indianapolis where she works as a residential organizer. Reading and writing poetry became lifelines for  her during years of accompanying her husband through a difficult illness. After his death, her writing became a vessel keeping her afloat in the grief. She enjoys gardening, ceramics, and photography, and looks for ways to balance the acute seriousness of the current climate with playfulness.

Teresa Pruitt writes: I am a female Hoosier. Odd as it may seem, I am very acquainted with many tools: hammers, screw drivers, wrenches, miter boxes, levels, ladders, shovels, hoes, wheelbarrows, tillers, sandpaper, mud, paint, pans, skillets, spatulas, thread, needles, yarn, piano, guitar, ukulele. A numerous variety of tools have been in my hands and given insight, instruction, and creation to the brain that thrives in my head. Last year, I picked up an old tool that was new to me: Pen and Paper. I've never taken time to enjoy the many benefits reading and writing bring. I am slowly entering this vast place for creation and expression.

Jacky Pugh grew up in Liverpool and ended up in Cornwall, the far southwest. She worked as a nurse and teacher, and recently retired from full time work, She is finding more time to focus on poetry, arts and crafts, but has always written poems and loved reading poetry and learning about it.

Levi Rinker is a slave to the man; trading away his mere existence "*all for the betterment of society*," or so he tells himself. Geesh! What a  martyr! You can find this rat stuck in the 9-5 race wearing a cheerleading skirt for local government and clicking his tap shoes to a revitalizing beat downtown. After work, he puts on a ridiculous cape and turns into the Art Director for A Town Center, a local artist co-op he co-founded with his partner Sonia. Under this umbrella, they scholarship yearly artist assistantships, host First Friday gallery openings, offer painting and printmaking classes, kids' camps, movie nights, and musical/theatrical events to the community. They also host a really awesome monthly poetry night, which is probably what got him a spot in this journal, if we really want to address the elephant in the room.

David Schloss was born in Brooklyn and educated at Columbia University, The University of Southern California Cinema School, Brooklyn College (BA), and The Iowa Writers Workshop (MFA). He taught at the University of Cincinnati and Miami University (Ohio), retiring as Emeritus Professor of English. He has five full-length poetry collections: *The Beloved, Sex Lives of the Poor and Obscure, Group Portrait from Hell, Reports from*  *Babylon and Beyond, The Heartbeat as an Ancient Instrument,* three chapbooks: *Legends*, *Greatest Hits*, and *Behind the Eyes,* as well as scores of poems published in literary journals and anthologies.

Mary Sexson is the author of *103 in the Light, Selected Poems 1996-200* (Restoration Press, 2004) and coauthor of *Company of Women, New and Selected Poems*, (Chatter House Press, 2013). A 3-time Pushcart Prize nominee, her poetry appears or is forthcoming in *Flying Island*, *New Verse News*, *The Globetrotter's Companion*, *The World We Live(d) In*, *Hoosier Lit*, *Last Stanza Poetry Journal*, *Laureate*, *High Veld Poetry Review, and Anti-Heroin Chic,* among others. Her poetry is part of the INverse Poetry Archive, a collection of poetry by Indiana poets, housed at the Indiana State Library.

Paul Smith is a civil engineer who has worked in the construction racket for many years. He has traveled all over the place and met lots of people. Some have enriched his life. Others made him wish he or they were all dead. He likes writing poetry and fiction. He also likes Newcastle Brown Ale. If you see him, buy him one. His poetry and  fiction have been published in *Convergence, Missouri Review, Literary Orphans,* and other lit mags.

Jeffrey Spahr-Summers is a former Commercial Photographer. He  has been experimenting with photography since he was a teenager. While much if his current work is highly colorful, black & white photography remains closer to his heart. His work can be seen on his website jeffreyspahrsummers.com.

Michael E. Strosahl was born and raised in Moline, Illinois, just blocks from the Mississippi River. He has written poetry since youth. After moving to Tipton, Indiana, he participated in a poetry reading on a dare at the Barnes & Noble in Westfield, Indiana, 2001. He then became active in

the Indiana poetry scene, becoming involved in what is now known as the Poetry Society of Indiana. He traveled the state in search of small groups that met in living rooms, libraries, and coffee houses, and he started groups in communities where he found none. He served the PSI as Membership Chair and eventually as President. In 2018, he relocated to Jefferson City, MO, beginning his search anew for kindred spirits to inspire and draw energy from. He currently co-hosts a monthly critique group in the capital city and is a member of Last Stanza Poetry Association.

Diana Thoresen is a Russian-Australian writer who works on free energy research and development. She is a Managing Editor/Cover Artist for the world's first multilingual anthology in 22 languages, *Voracious Polyglots.*

Theresa Timmons is a storyteller, gardener, dog lover, and mischievous "rider-of-roller-coasters" grandmother. When she is not playing with playdough or dancing in a tutu with the grandkids, she does a little writing. Theresa was a humor columnist for the *Anderson Herald* for ten years, and is a member of the Last Stanza Poetry Association.

Mary Kay Turner lives and works in the thriving Midwestern metropolis of Indianapolis. The craft of her life is propelled by the quadrifold values of meaningful work, intimate friendships, a deep inner life, and the sustaining power of creativity. And her cat. Don't forget the cat. This is her first published poem.

David Vancil retired from Indiana State University, where he taught composition and literature courses in the English Department and was the rare books librarian. He conducted the usual research as an academic, but his first love was writing—particularly poetry. His works have been published in small journals and a few anthologies. *The Homesick Patrol* is his longest collection of poems.

The Art School Baby, Night Photo, and *Moon Walking* are poetry chapbooks. He lives with his wife, three cats, and a dog.

Rp Verlaine lives in New York City. He has an MFA in creative writing  from City College. He taught in New York Public schools for many years. His first volume of poetry, *Damaged by Dames & Drinking,* was published in 2017 and another, *Femme Fatales, Movie Starlets & Rockers* in 2018. A set of three e-books titled *Lies from the Autobiography* were published from 2018 to 2020. His newest book, *Imagined Indecencies,* will be published in winter 2021.

Melody Wang currently resides in sunny Southern California with her dear husband. In her free time, she dabbles in piano composition and also enjoys hiking, baking, and playing with her dogs. She is a reader for *Sledgehammer Lit,* and can be found on Twitter @MelodyOfMusings.

Anne Marie Holwerda Warner is a Chicago carpenter's daughter perched in Kalamazoo, Michigan. Her poetry is published in *Indefinite Space, The Bitchin' Kitsch, Global Poemic, Harbinger Asylum, Impossible Task, Earth & Altar, The Hour, Moonchild, Ghost City Review* and *Q/A Poetry.*

Kim Watanabe is a physical therapist and visual artist whose first foray into the world of poetry began in Mr. Bennett's 8th-grade creative writing class in Kalamazoo. Now a resident of Indianapolis, she is coming out of the closet as an adult writer/poet in this journal with the steadfast support of a small posse of fellow writers.

James Eric Watkins has held everything in his hands from a carpenter's hammer to the pages Plato and Homer. He was first accepted by *Poetry Motel* in late 2002. Tragedy struck in 2009, and he suffered a massive heart attack that resulted in bypass surgery. James was forced to accept his newfound limitations in 2010 and step down as Lead Library Clerk at Ivy Tech Community College in Madison, Indiana. In 2012, he published his last piece as one of North America's emerging voices in poetry. After an eight-year hiatus, in 2020, James finally began to publish his work once again and has steadily done so since that time.

Liz Whiteacre is the author of *Hit the Ground.* Her poetry has appeared in *Disability Studies Quarterly, Wordgathering, Kaleidoscope,* and other magazines. Whiteacre is an assistant professor of English at the University of Indianapolis where she teaches creative writing, publishing, and advises Etchings Press.

Rita Yager is a nurse/teacher/photographer who writes about marginalized, at risk, and special needs populations. Poetry is her vehicle for delivering words about things that most people are afraid to admit that they feel, hopes her words give a voice that offers comfort and inclusion. She's been writing for fifty years, but only began submitting poetry after age sixty-five. She loves to write about relationships, nature, whimsy, and children.

Judy Young is a lifelong Elwood poet and member of Last Stanza Poetry Association, the Poetry Society of Indiana, and the National Federation of State Poetry Societies. She is married with five children, nine grandbabies, and seven great-grandchildren. She is the author of *Wild Wood* and *Moonset,* and has been published in *Tipton Poetry Journal, Indiana Voice Journal,* and in several

anthologies and other journals. She is a nature advocate and tree enthusiast.

Andrena Zawinski's poetry has received accolades for lyricism, form,  spirituality, and social concern. It has appeared in *Artemis, Blue Collar Review, Progressive Magazine, The Dallas Review, Aeolian Harp, Rattle, Verse Daily,* and elsewhere. Her latest collection is *Landings.* She has two previous award-winning books: *Something About* and *Traveling in Reflected Light,* with a fourth collection, *Born Under the Influence,* forthcoming in 2022.

Joyce Zephyrin is a member of Last Stanza Poetry Association, Poetry Society of Indiana, and AFSPS. She is the author of *Shadows on the Land* and *Turning Toward Home.* She has been published in *Hanover College's Hill Thoughts, Indiana Voice Journal,* and in anthologies. She worked for many years as a librarian, newspaper correspondent, and for magazines. A mother and grandmother, she serves as a CASA volunteer for children in need of services.